Days in the Life of a Sufi

RAZIUDDIN AQUIL is Associate Professor, Department of History, University of Delhi. He was previously Fellow in History, Centre for Studies in Social Sciences, Calcutta. His voluminous writings on Sufis and many other aspects of medieval Indian history have been read and appreciated by many. He is the author of *The Muslim Question: Understanding Islam and Indian History* (2017); *Lovers of God: Sufism and the Politics of Islam in Medieval India* (2017) and *Sufism, Culture and Politics: Afghans and Islam in Medieval North India* (2007).

Days in the Life of a Sufi

101 ENCHANTING STORIES OF WISDOM

RAZIUDDIN AQUIL

PAN

First published 2020 by Pan
an imprint of Pan Macmillan Publishing India Private Limited
707, Kailash Building,
26, K. G. Marg, New Delhi – 110 001
www.panmacmillan.co.in

Pan Macmillan, The Smithson, 6 Briset Street, London EC1M 5NR
Associated companies throughout the world
www.panmacmillan.com

ISBN 978-93-89109-68-9

3 5 7 9 8 6 4 2

Typeset in Guardi LT Std by R. Ajith Kumar, New Delhi
Printed and bound in India by Replika Press Pvt. Ltd.

To

Mr Susanta Ghosh

(Susanta Babu)

CONTENTS

PREFACE

Sufism is a vibrant spiritual movement within Islam. It has several strands which have developed across centuries and in different parts of the world. Originating in 8th-century Iraq with precedents even earlier in the times of Prophet Muhammad himself, Sufi traditions grew as part of a powerful mystical movement and spread to all corners of the known world. Central to this is the complete, even obsessive, love and devotion for God and to achieve a blissful mystical union with Him. This they called *ishq-i haqiqi*, true love for God, compared to *ishq-i majazi*, desire for this-worldly objects of love. They aspired to achieve this through a systematic cultivation of the soul, purifying the lower-self, and dedicating themselves in the service of all the creations of God. Service to humanity was considered the best form of worship. This was done through charitable endeavours, blessings and benediction for which large numbers of people throng to Sufi shrines, *mazar*s and *dargah*s even today. Many of the visitors and devotees to these places are not Muslims, but they have faith in the spiritual powers of Sufi saints. It is believed by the visitors that the Sufis have achieved nearness to God. This belief prevails even in times when Islam is stigmatized because of terror and violence in its name. This means that the followers understand the distinction between the humanism of Sufi spirituality and brutalities involved in violent political abuses of Islam.

Sufis also adopted spiritual practices which were beyond the juridically recommended Islamic obligations. This would often run them into trouble with the custodians of Islam. Sufis defended themselves as true followers of the path of the Prophet in their complete and unconditional submission to the will of God. They expressed these through their voluminous writings, discourses and powerful poetry. The latter included a systematically developed art form – often blending song, music and dance, which also appealed to popular taste and catered to the need for some music in one's life. Sufis recognized that only a heartless being will have no sense of music.

Wherever Sufis went they got themselves embedded in local culture and spoke of their love for God in the language the people understood. In the subcontinent, from as early as the eleventh century onwards, they sang and preached in Punjabi in Punjab, Dakani in Deccan, Bengali in Bengal. In the cow-belt of Hindustan, they spoke in Hindi and from the 15th century onwards avoided eating beef in deference to the sentiments of sections of people. They also composed their poetry of love in a genre called *premakhyan*, the best example of which is *Padmavat* of Malik Muhammad Jaisi. This latter text was in the news in recent times, as a Hindi film based on it could not handle the intricate entanglements of literature, spirituality and politics in history and the present leading to a caricature of the original poetry. In the charged political atmosphere, looking at Sufi *premakhyan* texts, cynics may wonder how is it that Sufis wrote such exquisite poetry of love despite being Muslims, especially as the latter are increasingly and erroneously being identified as terrorists or their sympathizers.

The 101 Sufi stories recounted in this collection unravel many dimensions of Islamic spirituality. The touching images of Sufis, their practices and teachings serve as important lessons relevant to our troubled times. The believers simply need to be sincere in their devotion to God and be kind and respectful to all His creations, including human beings, animals and plants. Readers of this book can straightaway move from here to savour the stories from the lives of the Sufis. Those interested in knowing the background and contexts can also read the introduction to the book. An epilogue at the end further summarizes the significance of Sufi anecdotes found in the literatures of Sufis themselves.

I take this opportunity to thank my friends and colleagues who have heard me narrating Sufi anecdotes for nearly three decades now: Deeksha Bhardwaj, Partha Chatterjee, David Curley, Amit Dey, Jack Hawley, Mazhar Hussain, Bharati Jagannathan, Anshu Malhotra, Sanal Mohan, Tilottama Mukherjee, Santosh Rai, Yousuf Saeed, Arupjyoti Saikia, Vipul Singh, and Chitralekha Zutshi.

I am grateful to my publisher friends Mimi Choudhury and Prasun Chatterjee who have continuously encouraged me to work on this collection, of Sufi tales meant for the benefits to the hearts of the people, through dissonant times, and always. Susanta Ghosh (Susanta Babu), a distinguished academic administrator in Kolkata, has for long been an ardent advocate of the value of my research and writings for understanding Islam in the Indian subcontinent with all its fantastic peculiarities and regional diversities. I present these stories as a gift to him, cherishing memories of times we have spent together.

Raziuddin Aquil
University of Delhi

AN INTRODUCTION TO SUFISM

Early Sufism

Humanistic Sufi practices have a long history. It has two broad aspects: love for God and service to humanity. These two features are central to a large number of anecdotes, including tales of miracles, narrated in this book. Together these stories reveal that Sufism was not merely an abstract mystical philosophy, but it played crucial social and cultural roles in bringing together a vast diversity of people to shape a society that respected multiplicity, central to which was a loving devotion for God who can be accessed through the mediation of a Sufi saint. Thus, a large number of people flocked to them for blessings and benediction.

Sufism emerged as a significant religious and intellectual movement in Iraq in the latter half of the 9th century CE. Despite oppositions and hostilities over its many complex ideas and doctrines as well as crucial social and political interventions, this path of devotion went on to enjoy a wide following and considerable political clout in Islamic societies through the Middle Ages. The critical early phase of Sufism from the 9th to 12th centuries not only saw its spread to a vast geographical expanse, with regions of Khurasan and Transoxania emerging as major centres of activities, but also witnessed the formulation of Sufi discipline and practices. These comprised the centrality of the love for Allah, following the path of the Prophet, spiritual practices including a blend of music, poetry and dance called *sama*, miracles and sainthood. This was the period when many forms of Islam – legal schools (*mazahib*) and sects (*firqas*) – emerged and there were bitter contestations on the most righteous one which could lead Muslims through the straight path of Allah as guided by Prophet Muhammad. Despite appearing to be withdrawn from the ways of the world, the Sufis too were important participants in much of the debate on what it meant to be a pious Muslim.[1]

With key figures like, Abu Sa'id al-Kharraz (died circa 899), Abu'l Husayn al-Nuri (died 907-08) and Abu'l Qasim al-Junayd (died 910), located in Baghdad in the latter half of the 9th century, Sufism grew as a distinct mode of piety. It included meditation for experiential knowledge of God (*ma'rifat*) and his unity (*tauhid*), spiritual experience of the passing away of self-consciousness (*fana*), maintaining sobriety (*sahw*), despite extraordinary feelings of being close to God, and showing the way to others through the mystic path (*tariqat*). Despite occasional setbacks such as the shocking execution of al-Husayn ibn Mansur al-Hallaj in 922, which had more to do with a political intervention that went awry than merely spiritual utterances of heretical nature, Sufis emerged in a big way. They were also going to travel all around the Muslim dominion and beyond.

Large swathes of territories in Iran and Central Asia were already home to a vibrant tradition of mystical thought and practice. Even though the term Sufi was not yet used in distant locations like Khurasan and Transoxania, many features were common to the mystic fraternities of 'metropolitan' Baghdad and those of these 'provincial' centres. However, by the beginning of the 10th century the term Sufi had begun to be used in all these areas and distinctions and differences of approach were reflected in a perceptive remark of a contemporary observer: 'Sufism of Khurasan is practice and no talk; Sufism of Baghdad is talk and no practice; Sufism in Basra is talk as well as practice; and Sufism in Egypt is no talk and no practice!'[2] It is interesting to see that some stereotypes were already beginning to emerge.

The 10th century saw Baghdad-style Sufism develop firm roots in Khurasan and Transoxania in the east and around this time it possibly spread to Iberia in the west. The process included 'merger' and 'fusion' between local and regional forms of devotion and configuring of a more 'cosmopolitan urban' synthesis, as in the case of the 'absorption' of the Path of Blame (Malamatiyya) which was outside the ambit of Islam during initial days, by Sufism.[3] The 10th century also witnessed interesting struggles between the ascendancy of Iraqi Sufism and its compromises in the regions. This process eventually led to the formation of communities with distinct spiritual lineages (*silsila*s), doctrines and practices built around Sufi masters (*shaikhs/murshid*s) and their close disciples (*murid*s) lodged in hospices (*khanqahs/ribat*s). The rise of such tightly-knit communities of Sufis got entangled with the cult of popular saints in Islam. Even though many of their activities were viewed with suspicion by theologians (*ulama*) and they were attacked by antagonists of different hues, the Sufis, as friends (*auliya*) of God, came to enjoy an exalted status and became major social and political players through the 11th and 12th centuries.

The Sufi fraternities themselves guarded their activities and articulated their beliefs through a variety of literature, pointing to significant intellectual connections and lineages in the building up of their traditions. The specialized literature highlighted the primacy of the Sufi mode of piety over all other forms of religiosity in early Islam. This corpus drew the normative boundaries of 'true Sufism' to distinguish it from 'fake', 'false' or 'misguided' forms of mystical movements. It also served to preserve and propagate the legacy of the early masters and called for solidarity within 'Sufi communities through shared discourses of theoretical and practical guidance'.[4] The vast composition and rapid dispersal of Sufi literature may also be understood in the context of Sufism responding to the questions raised by, and adjusting to the pressures from, not only the rationalist Mu'tazila and the legitimist Shi'as, but also the extremely competitive and watchful juridical schools (*mazahib*) within Sunnite Islam.

Prophetic tradition refers to three dimensions of Islam: *islam*, *iman* and *ihsan; islam*, or submission, was forced by the jurists (*mufti*s and *qazi*s); *iman*, or faith, was preached by the theologians; and *ihsan*, the propensity to do beautiful things, was practiced by Sufis, making them appear as the best among the Muslims. This third dimension, *ihsan*, constituted the heart of religion marked by sincerity, love, virtue, and perfection, qualities which the Sufis aspired for.[5]

Typically, the Sufis began their quest by shunning all the anxieties of attachment to this world, whether private or public. They called for soul searching, remembrance of God beyond the ritual prayers of the mosques, meditation in solitude and wandering around as dervishes to the Muslim cities and non-Muslim or semi-Islamized hinterlands. At the end of it, they came back with claims of personally experiencing the truth of Islam, of the loving God and the righteousness of the path of the Prophet – strengthening here the position of the Sunnite *ulama* and the theologians. As religious exemplars, then, the Sufis were supposed to guide the Muslims, ignoring, or tolerating human weaknesses, and also bring non-Muslims to the fold of Islam. Thus, Sufism was a major strand in Islam before it came to the Indian subcontinent.

Coming of Sufism to the Subcontinent

Of the Sufi orders that had emerged, four of them enjoyed considerable importance in medieval and early modern India from the 13th to the end of 18th century. Two of these orders, Chishtis and Suhrawardis, flourished in the Sultanate period, while the other two, Qadiri and Naqshbandi, became significant in the Mughal era. Over time, smaller branches and sub-branches of these spiritual lineages such as Firdausis and Shattaris spread in different regions and localities. To start with, the living Sufi master guided followers or visitors at his hospice, but later the shrines (*mazar*s and *dargah*s) of Sufis of previous generations became important and grew into places of pilgrimage, eventually carving a whole sacred geography of Sufism at that site, called *wilayat*. This notion of *wilayat* involved a lot of struggle and competition for control of territory, followers and resources, as we shall further see below.

What distinguished Sufism from other forms of Islam was its belief that a human soul could achieve union with God, a belief formulated in the doctrine of *wahdat-ul-wujud* which means unity of existence, or monism as a reality, by the 13th-century Iberian Sufi master Ibn-i-Arabi. This doctrine often brought Sufis into conflict with Islamic orthodoxy represented by Sunni Hanafite *ulama* or theologians of the Delhi Sultanate.[6] The latter believed that God was unique and, therefore, to suggest that a human soul could achieve union with God was to imply that there was no distinction between God and human beings. This was different from the monotheistic notion of unity of God, *tauhid*, which implied a duality – God and His creations. It is for this reason that Sufis were occasionally attacked and persecuted by the *ulama* or their followers.

Sufis were also targeted by the *ulama* for their alleged indifference to formal religious practices such as regular congregational prayers (*namaz/salat*), instead focusing on meditations and spiritual exercises which included devotional music, as part of *zikr*, or remembrance of God. The legitimacy of listening to music, in the form of *sama* or *qawwali*, was a major source of confrontation between the *ulama* and the Sufis. Despite opposition from sections of the *ulama*, the Sufis' contribution to the spread of poetry and music have been significant in the Indian milieu. Sufi orders such as the Chishtis used song and dance techniques for concentration and for creating spiritual ecstasy. The Sufis also played a significant role in the growth and development of the vernacular literature such as Bengali, Deccani, Hindi, Punjabi, Urdu, and several others. By contrast, the court culture facilitated the spread and dominance of Persian as the official language of power and government, while the role of Arabic was mostly reduced to theology. Sufi traditions, therefore, contributed greatly to the development of both Indian folk and classical culture.

The belief in *wahdat-ul-wujud* and several forms or techniques of meditation brought the Sufis spiritually very close to certain strands of non-Muslim religious traditions in the Indian subcontinent. For example, Advaita Hinduism claimed that *atma* (a human soul) and *parmatma* (God) were one and the same, a theory similar to *wahdat-ul-wujud*. Similarly, the Sufis found much to learn from bodily practices in Hindu spiritual disciplines such as Yoga, which influenced their techniques of meditation. Mention maybe made here of the similarities of the popular Yogic practice of *pranayama,* breath control, with the more spectacular Sufi practice of *chilla-i-ma'kus*, hanging oneself upside down from a branch of a tree overlooking a well located in the courtyard of a mosque, though generally conducted in private and in the darkness of night.[7]

If Sufis learnt from non-Muslim traditions, the latter were also powerfully affected by the principles of Islam as represented by Sufi saints. In the teachings of Sant Kabir and Guru Nanak one can see the clear imprint of Sufi Islam. The criticism of idol worship and rituals, emphasis on equality, devotion to one God, are all to be traced to Sufism. In the case of Sikhism, whole sections of the Guru Granth Saheb essentially consist of Sufi poetry. Sufism's greatest contribution to Indian culture is the example it set in the field of religious and cultural co-existence. Sufi orders showed that Muslim and non-Muslim religious traditions could flourish side-by-side and learn from each other.

The closeness to non-Muslim traditions helped Sufis play an important role in conversion and Islamization, even if many of them did not work with an explicit agenda of this sort. Yet, the presence of Sufis was the main factor in the conversion of large sections of the subcontinent's population to Islam. To start with, Sufi institutions, *khanqahs/dargahs*, became centres where Muslims and non-Muslims gathered for worship, meditation or spiritual experience and sought blessings and benediction from the Sufi masters. The process of conversion started with devotion towards a particular Sufi, leading to the emergence of syncretic sects, symbolizing only half or partial conversion. Eventually, there emerged communities of Muslims who professed Islam formally, but continued with their practice of local customs and traditions, which were condemned by the puritanical, reformist Islamists. Reformist and revivalist movements have gained ground particularly from 18th-19th centuries onwards.

The *ulama*'s attitude towards the Sufis was generally hostile. They considered many of the Sufi ideas and practices as heretical from the point of view of their own interpretation of the *shari'at,* or Islamic law. Even as the *ulama* were more concerned with guarding orthodoxy than spreading Islam and their contact with non-Muslims was limited, the role played by the Sufis in conversion and Islamization was not counted as important by the *ulama.* The latter thought that the quality of Islam practiced and preached by the Sufis was inadequate and inferior. In fact, the *ulama* attacked many of the Sufi practices, condemning them to be un-Islamic. For this purpose, they often tried to use political power also.

It is generally suggested that the relationship between Sufi orders and the state was distant. Orders like the Chishtis refused to accept money or support from the ruler. They believed that involvement in politics led to materialism and worldliness which they wanted to avoid. However, this attitude varied from order to order and between Sufis within an order also. Whereas the Chishtis recommended aloofness from the state, the Suhrawardis had no qualms about associating with the Sultan's court. Even the Chishtis of the Deccan accepted patronage of the state. The Naqshbandis and the Qadiris were also known for their political involvement in the Mughal period, though the representatives of these two *silsilas* displayed remarkable divergence in their approach to contemporary social and political issues.

Sources and Historiography

The vast Indian Sufi literature in Persian and vernaculars includes (i) *malfuzat* or discourses of a Sufi compiled by a disciple, *murid*, generally in the lifetime of the Sufi himself; (ii) *maktubat*, or letters, written by a Sufi to his disciples; (iii) mystical treatises on Sufism prepared by a Sufi shaikh; (iv) compilations of Sufi poetry of love, of which *premakhyan* took a fascinating vernacular form; (v) *tazkiras*, or hagiographies of Sufis, compiled generally after their death and comprised interesting legends and anecdotes, including miracle stories (*karamat*). Important information on Sufi activities may also be found in court-chronicles and general histories, particularly on matters relating to the Sufis' relations with the rulers. While over the past century many studies have taken place on the history and trends in Sufism, many themes remain unexplored which are finding their way through the works of recent scholars such as Scott Kugle and Nile Green.

In what follows, some of the representative writings on the perennial debate on what were the different roles the Sufis played in medieval India will be explored. Of particular interest is the question whether the Sufis were interested in conversion and Islamization. Sufi traditions have celebrated, since, at least mid-14th century, the image of leading Sufi masters as Islamizers in various parts of the subcontinent. They also claim that the Sufi shaikhs actually facilitated Muslim conquests of the regions and thus contributed to the expansion of Islam in India. Modern scholars have read such assertions in Sufi literature such as the *malfuzat*, 'discourses' of a Sufi, and *tazkiras*, biographical dictionaries, in terms of their context such as the political situation, location and viewpoint of the authors and the purpose of writing these texts. This has led to contesting views of Sufism in India.

The existing formulations on Sufism can be summarized in two broad counter-positions. It is suggested in the first set of literature that the medieval Indian Sufis kept themselves away from politics and government of their times for they believed that involvement in politics led to materialism and worldliness, which they wished to avoid. Thus, Sufi saints of the orders like the Chishtis not only refused to accept money or land grants from the rulers, but also declined to make a person their disciple till he had left government service, and sold all his possessions and distributed the amount amongst the poor. It is asserted in these writings that in no form contact with the state was tolerated. Further, the abhorrence to politics compelled the Sufis to stay away from the centres of political influence and establish their hospice (*jama'atkhana* or *khanqah*) in the localities inhabited by low-caste Hindus. The spiritually hungry and depressed classes were amazed by the shining example of Islamic brotherhood and egalitarianism as reflected in the activities of the hospice such as the *langar* (free kitchen). This fascinating image of the true Islam represented by the Sufis paved the way for a revolution marked by large-scale conversion of the teeming lower classes. However, it is also emphasized that the Sufis, in general, and the Chishtis, in particular, were tolerant towards non-Muslim religious traditions. They were, therefore, indifferent towards conversion. In fact, it is noted that there was no evidence of even a single case of conversion in the mystic records of the Delhi Sultanate. Such arguments, repeated at regular intervals, could be found in the numerous writings of scholars like Carl Ernst, Mohammad Habib, Yusuf Husain, Bruce Lawrence, K.A. Nizami, S.A.A. Rizvi and I.H. Siddiqui, among others. [8]

In sharp contrast to above assertions, a number of other scholars have observed that the Sufis, including the 'great' Chishtis of the Sultanate period, did take part in politics. Some of them visited the reigning Sultans. Others avoided visiting the Sultan's court perhaps because they considered it below their dignity to go to the court and follow its rituals. A section of them may have also felt that a tactical 'on stage' distance from the rulers was advisable for the reconciliation of a large majority of, often hostile, non-Muslim population of loosely conquered territories. Thus, the Sufis came to settle in centres of political influence or in areas already made sacred by non-Muslim religious traditions. Other strategic places they chose to stay were the much-trodden trade routes. Certainly, mainstream Sufi orders such as the influential Chishtis, Suhrawardis and Naqshbandis were against the idea of settling in forests or at lonely places. They participated in the Muslim campaigns for political conquests, which were often portrayed as fighting *jihad* or holy wars against the *kafir*s or infidels. Some also contributed to the lasting Muslim control of newly conquered territories, in the process carving out a *wilayat* or spiritual domain for themselves. In course of time, Sufi explorers could settle down as landlords as well, beginning generally with the revenue-free land grants with hereditary rights (*madad-i-ma'sh* or *in'am*) and then going on to become owners of these lands. These are not simply a matter of opinion, as a great deal of evidence has been marshalled in support of the above propositions in the numerous writings of, among others, Muzaffar Alam, Simon Digby and Richard Eaton.

Simultaneously, the emerging shrines or *dargah*s served as one of the major nodal points for interaction between Muslims and the non-Muslim population of the area. In some cases, a long process of Islamic acculturation took place around the shrines, leading eventually to the conversion of non-Muslims to Islam and formation of local Muslim communities. This process was often resisted and challenged by leaders of non-Muslim religious traditions. Sufi literature highlights the accounts of encounters, debates and dialogues between Sufis, on the one hand, and Brahmins and Yogis, on the other. Further, the competing claims to authority in a given territory, where spiritual power of the Sufis matched the sway of the Sultans' armed strength, could lead to violent conflict. Mutual respect and collaboration between Sufis and rulers were however not uncommon, even as the guardians of Sunni Muslim orthodoxy, the *ulama*, tried to use their occasional differences to advance their own 'Islamic' agenda. In this book, we encounter stories that depict all these varied themes and their interconnections which portray the fascinating array of negotiations, contestations and accommodations. The short cryptic stories which follow in this book represent this gamut of experiences, and these can be understood through two broad themes which we will explore now: the arguments over the authoritative position of Sufis in medieval India, which often reflected in political interventions and conflicts, and the question of Sufis' role in conversion and Islamization in the Indian environment.

Miracle as a Source of Sufi Shaikh's Authority

There are a large number of anecdotes in Sufi literature about the Sufis' confrontations with their opponents: opposition, disrespect and abusive epithets used by the Sultans, *ulama* (Muslim religious scholars) and other people of worldly influence, often led to the provocation of the *jalal* (wrath) of the Sufi shaikhs. In such situations, the Sufi's miracles served, in a way, as a weapon to overawe, subdue, terrorize and occasionally to even annihilate the opponents. The curse of the shaikh often 'caused' sudden and painful death of the antagonist.[9] In some cases, the shaikh left the issue to be decided by God and went to the extent of leaving the place. For instance, the Sufi master Khwaja Muinuddin Sijzi (died 1236) wanted his *khalifa* (spiritual successor), Khwaja Qutbuddin Bakhtiyar Kaki (died 1235) to relocate from Delhi to Ajmer in order to avoid a conflict with the religious leader of the Delhi Sultanate, Shaikh-ul-Islam Najmuddin Sughra. Bakhtiyar Kaki, however, had to stay back due to an immense public and political demand.[10]

Similarly, Khwaja Nizamuddin Auliya (died 1325) had left for Ajodhan to avoid a meeting with Sultan Jalaluddin Firuz Khalji (ruled 1290-96).[11] Later he is said to have remarked that he would leave the place if Sultan Alauddin Khalji (ruled 1296-1316) continued to disturb him.[12] The Sultan's hostility came to an end only after the shaikh announced in no uncertain terms that he was not interested in matters of government and would prefer to pray for the welfare of the Muslims and their king.[13] There are also episodes in which the adversary is forgiven altogether. For example, Sultan Muhammad bin Tughluq (ruled 1325-51) did not face the wrath of the Sufi Nasiruddin Mahmud Chiragh-i-Dehli (died 1356). The Sultan was said to have harassed the shaikh at a particular stage of his career.[14]

The source of this conflict lay in the *wilayat* of the shaikh, as Simon Digby has shown, and this encroached for all practical purposes, the territorial authority of the ruler. If a major shaikh laid claim to *wilayat* or spiritual rule over a territory, which the king held by the force of his arms, then it was below the dignity of the shaikh to be seen under the sovereign's patronage. The shaikh, thus, refused to accept grants from the Sultan and attend his court (*darbar*), which involved the observance of court etiquette designed to emphasize the supremacy of the monarch. Alternatively, the shaikh would not permit the ruler to visit his hospice so as to avoid receiving him with the same politeness, as was the lot of the common visitors.[15] The *wilayat* of the shaikh had a direct influence on the political events and material destiny of the realm. The shaikh's ability to bestow kingship, his role as the protector of the people in times of crisis and as the healer of the sick made him extremely popular. Of particular note was the Sufi's massive following among the courtiers and the soldiers not unlike the following they command even now from politicians and other significant people in contemporary times.[16] Thus, the Sufi's indifference towards the rituals of the Sultan's court, his refusal to allow the reigning king to visit his hospice and his encroachment into the power base of the ruler, that is, the nobles and the ordinary soldiers, constituted a threat to the political authority. The conspiracy against Sultan Jalaluddin Khalji with Sidi Muwallih or Sayyidi Maula as the figurehead of a rebellion is a case in point. It was nipped in the bud with the brutal killing of the shaikh. However, it was reported that a terrible wind blew on the day of the shaikh's execution followed by drought and famine in Delhi and its neighbourhood.[17] Shaikh

Abdul Haqq Muhaddis, a leading scholar of Sufism in Mughal India, says that the Qalandars of Shaikh Abu Bakr Tusi killed Sidi Muwallih. The divine retribution in the form of a terrifying wind on the day of the execution forced Jalaluddin Khalji to have faith in the Sufis.[18]

In these conflicts the *ulama* sided with the ruler and questioned the violation of the *shari'at* by the shaikh in matters such as listening to music (*sama*)[19] and refusal to perform the congregational prayers.[20] The Sufi, in turn, looked down upon the *ulama* and advised young job seekers against joining the service of the king. In Sufi literature in most contests, the Sufi is shown to have emerged victorious, sometimes by establishing his superior knowledge of the *shari'at*, on other occasions by his healing and levitatory activities, and, on yet others by 'causing' the death of the enemies. The message that came out from the Sufi circle was aloud and clear: the person who provoked the shaikh was uprooted.[21]

Further, the incumbent Sufi never wanted the visiting shaikh of a rival *silsila* to stay in his territory for long. Threatened as he was, he often gave a symbolic indication that the traveller should move on revealing intense competition and control among diverse Sufi traditions. The control of areas also worked on mutual legitimacy as Sufi Fariduddin Ganj-i-Shakar once told a traveller seeking intercession for his travel from Ajodhan to Multan: 'From here to such and such a reservoir is the frontier of Bahauddin Zakariya, beyond which is in his charge' and the blessings of the two saints in their respective *wilayat* will ensure a safe journey.[22] This incident also demonstrates how closely the notion of spiritual geography could parallel that of political authority and Richard Eaton rightly notes that this is one of the ways that religious influence and political power were fused together.[23] There always existed tension between the Sufis about safeguarding their *wilayat* and the differences often came to the fore with the rival parties trying to belittle each other in different ways.

Besides, there are numerous anecdotes in the literature of the Delhi Sultanate concerning the bestowal of kingship by the Sufi saints upon a person of their choice, which was usual in a society without a strong tradition of primogeniture and usurpation of power was common.[24] According to an anecdote, as a young slave in Bukhara, the future Sultan Shamsuddin Iltutmish was sent to purchase some grapes. He lost the money on the way and started crying out of fear. Observing the child's predicament, a dervish bought some grapes for him and asked him to pledge that when he succeeded to the dominion, he would show respect to the holy men. The story goes that Iltutmish became a Sultan due to the grace of that dervish.[25] Later, Nizamuddin Auliya told his audience that Iltutmish had met Shahabuddin Suhrawardi and Auhaduddin Kirmani, and one of them had prophesied that he would become a king.[26]

The rulers' acceptance of the reports that they owed their power to the saint's blessings indicated their quest for legitimacy against precarious conditions of rule. On the other hand, the stories of conflict and collaboration – acting as king makers, offering prayers for the welfare of Muslims and their ruler – testify to the Sufis' interests in political matters. In earlier studies, denied mainly regarding the Chishtis, this political role of the Sufis has been illustrated clearly in recent studies with copious evidence.[27] The stories of miracles further confirm the Sufis' involvement in matters of political interest. As noted above, there were contestations between the Sufis themselves as well as those with the king and the *ulama*. In the resultant conflict, the monarch at times utilized the support of the *ulama* and that of the Sufis of a rival *silsila*. Among the weapons that the Sufi shaikh used was his miraculous power to eliminate the adversary. In the case of the differences between Sufi Nizamuddin Auliya and the Delhi Sultans, Qutbuddin Mubarak Shah Khalji (ruled 1316-20) and Ghiyasuddin Tughluq (ruled 1321-25), the Sultans were removed by the curse one by one. The saint's *jalal* affected even the populace, as his curse is believed to have caused famine and epidemic in the city.

If the curse of the Sufis caused destruction, their blessings (*barkat*) could also protect the people and their *wilayat* in times of crisis. Their role as the saviour is well illustrated in the accounts of the Mongol attacks, which shook the Muslim world for over a hundred years from the early-13th century to the mid-14th century.[28] Such episodes point to the limitations of military power, which made the people turn to the Sufis for succour. This also gave impetus to claims that the towns and cities would be destroyed if the *barkat* of the dervishes were stopped.[29] In fact, according to Nizamuddin Auliya, a certain Khwaja Karim used to boast that no infidel could capture Delhi so long as his grave existed there.[30]

Besides the problem of the Mongols, the Sufis were also approached for protection from certain malevolent supernatural beings such as the *pari*[31] and to destroy the *jinns* and the sickness arising due to their perceived presence.[32] Many references show that they recommended certain verses of the Qur'an as an antidote against their visitations.[33] Visits to the tombs of the Sufis, their relics, amulets (*t'awiz*) distributed by them, 'breathing' and 'touching' were considered to be effective healing means.[34] Apart from curing the sick, cases of revival of the dead at the hands of the Sufis are also reported. A performance of this miracle by Qutbuddin Bakhtiyar Kaki led to the conversion of thousands of non-Muslims to Islam.[35] We shall return to this theme in the next section.

Stories such as these created an aura around the personality of the Sufis. The defeat of the hostile *ulama* and their acceptance of the Sufi shaikh's paranormal power added to the latter's popularity and authoritative position in society.[36] Also, some Sufis had no qualms about 'advertising' their own extraordinary spiritual abilities. However, Nizamuddin Auliya detested such Sufis who sought to gain popularity by showcasing their miraculous powers. He felt that it was obligatory for the *auliya* (friends of God) to downplay their *karamat*, even as it was binding upon the *anbiya* (prophets) to display their *mu'ajizat* (miracles).[37]

In fact, it was humility – together with the performance of marvellous feats – that made the people venerate the Sufis. The relationship between the Sufis and their followers were seen in terms of mutual fidelity and aid. The people revered a shaikh and, in turn, were blessed with his patronage and protection. Fariduddin Ganj-i-Shakar is said to have left for Hansi as the people of the place were prevented from having an easy access to the shaikh in the capital city.[38] Later, he was reportedly told by a follower that he was keeping aloof from the people at Ajodhan.[39] Nizamuddin Auliya informed his audience that he was advised by a visitor to his *jama'atkhana*, probably a member of the *mardan-i-ghayb* (men of the unseen), to stay at Ghiyaspur in Delhi when the shaikh was contemplating to move to a lonely place.[40] When the Sufi Chiragh-i-Dehli expressed his desire to leave the city and settle at some small and desolate place, his *pir* commanded him to remain and work among the people.[41] The departure of a Sufi from a particular area was considered to be a bad omen. Nizamuddin, for instance, believed that the region of Punjab was secured from the Mongol onslaught because of the blessings of Fariduddin Ganj-i-Shakar. In the year when the shaikh departed from this world, the Mongols invaded and devastated the region.[42]

The Sufi shaikh's authoritative position in the society was contested not only by the Sultans and the *ulama,* but also by wandering Muslim mystics like the Qalandars and the non-Muslim Yogis on the basis of the shaikh's power and prestige. The Qalandars, visiting the *jama'atkhana,* often created problems and resorted to violence. In fact, several reports of murderous assaults either planned or actually carried out by the Qalandars on the Sufi shaikhs such as Fariduddin Ganj-i-Shakar, Nizamuddin Auliya and Chiragh-i-Dehli are to be found in the sources.[43] The episodes reveal not only the hostility of these groups to the Sufi shaikh but also that they were occasionally hired by the political opponents of the shaikh to eliminate him. Further, the stories tend to portray these wandering mystics as psychologically disturbed people.[44]

In contrast to the Qalandars, the visiting Yogis/ Brahmins/Sanyasis/Gurus of the Hindus tended to be less aggressive, or at least they are portrayed in the Sufi sources to be so. Some of them came to test the paranormal powers of the Sufis and were often simply over-awed by their exploits. In these anecdotes, the Sufi shaikh's superior miraculous abilities having been established, the visiting non-Muslim spiritual powerholder would embrace Islam and become a disciple to rise to the high status of a *wali* (disciple) in his own right. Alternatively, feeling humiliated he would take to his heels. In some cases, miraculous contests were held in which the non-Muslim spiritual leaders were said to have been defeated. Stories of the triumphs of the Sufi in such combats further aimed at legitimizing their claim to authority in the *wilayat*.

An important source of the Sufi's authority was his perceived ability to perform incredible feats. Many of these tales were narrated by no less an authority than the leading Chishti shaikh of Delhi, Nizamuddin Auliya. Subsequent narrators such as Chiragh-i-Dehli, Shaikh Jamali and Abdul Haqq Muhaddis not only related the episodes of miracles with added details, but also occasionally introduced new motifs into the existing tales. For all of them, miracle was an integral part of the Sufi discipline. Thus, the notion that the miracle stories were later concoctions by the shrewd keepers of the shrines who sought to exploit the credulity of the ignorant followers is not always true. On the contrary, the leading Sufis themselves believed that the *auliya* or the friends of God, who had followed the mystic path (*tariqat*) could acquire supernatural faculties. In their opinion, however, the mystics were expected to refrain from flaunting the power that they were supposed to have attained. However, sustained provocation from any antagonist or the miserable condition of a devotee could legitimately induce him to perform miracles, which manifested itself either in the form of *jalal* (curse) or *jamal* (grace).

Further, though many of the motifs of miracles were of universal or folkloric nature many Sufis were not only learned scholars of their time, but they also produced their discourses in Persian, itself a language of the elite. Therefore, the application of such terms as 'folk-belief' or 'popular-belief' are questionable as the Sufis themselves located their experiences and positions in the 'great' tradition of Islam – a tradition that was informed by the Qur'an, the Traditions of Prophet Muhammad, and examples from the lives of leading religious personalities of early Islam. The followers of the Sufis hoped to be successful both 'here' (in this world) and the 'hereafter' (in the next). By contrast, the accursed opponents of the shaikhs were not merely subdued, but also said to be despatched to hell. The public had the option to either submit to the authority of the Sufis and be 'rewarded' for it, or refuse to acknowledge the latter's charisma and sainthood, which could lead to calamity and destruction in society.

For K.A. Nizami, it was the broad and cosmopolitan outlook of the Sufis, marked by their belief in the unity of God and service to humanity, that brought about a social and cultural revolution of far-reaching consequences, removing mistrust and isolation and facilitating social and ideological rapproachments between communities. In Aziz Ahmad's appreciation of Sufi activities in Indian Hindu environment, the various orders began with hostility, passed through a phase of co-existence and culminated in tolerance. As the Sufis penetrated into Hindu society and began to attract converts to Islam, the Bhakti movements rose as a popular Hindu counter-challenge to the proselytizing pull of Sufi humanism. Similarly, Muzaffar Alam has shown with reference to the 18th-century Awadh how the Sufis, backed by their belief in *wahdat-ul-wujud*, or unity of being, adapted themselves to the surrounding environment, even as social identities existed with conflicting and contradictory pulls and the rulers were politically compelled to adopt a liberal and pragmatic approach. As Alam put it, even the most charismatic Sufis struggled in their endeavour to 'reconcile the irreconcilables'.

Conversion and Islamization

As indicated above, the missionary and proselytizing activities of the Sufis and their organizations have been noted in some modern writings. These include Islamization through large-scale immigration of foreign Muslims, conversion through the sword or political patronage and social liberation of lower-caste Hindus, who were attracted toward egalitarian Islam, represented by the Sufis.[45] Within contemporary Sufi writings and studies on them also, there is no single opinion. Some historians have explained the attitude towards conversion in terms of the general outlook of the particular *silsila* to which the Sufi belonged. Thus, the Chishtis are considered tolerant and accommodative and, therefore, disinterested in formal conversion while the Suhrawardis are mentioned to be orthodox, uncompromising and, keen to convert even if it meant use of force.[46] Some other scholars trace the difference to ideological positions maintained by particular shaikhs. It is argued that those who believed in *wahdat-ul-wujud* considering monism as a reality, were open-minded towards the Hindus, caring little or not at all about their conversion, while those who followed *wahdat-us-shuhud* arguing for the feeling of monism as a mystic experience distinct from reality, tended to be hostile to them and favoured forced conversion.[47] A third group of scholars think of conversion in terms of the long process of Islamic acculturation.[48] One of the best examples of this latter set of writing is Richard Eaton's work on slow and gradual process of Islamic acculturation, rather than any sudden 'conversion' by Sufi 'missionaries'. Eaton notes that both the terms used above, 'conversion' and 'missionaries', are uncritically derived from the 19th- and 20th-century Christian missionary movement in India and cannot be used for Sufi activities for a context like medieval Bijapur in the Deccan. Similarly, denying that conversion of non-Muslims was one of the primary objectives of Sufi activities in the medieval Indian environment, Carl Ernst notes that the 'Sufi as missionary' image was erroneously constructed and disseminated by three later sources: royal histories of the contemporary times, tribal and caste traditions incorporated in later hagiographies and British gazetteers, and 19th-century British concepts of Christian missions. There is a misfit between the image of the Sufis in later writings and 'the picture of Sufi discipline and practice as found in the early Sufi manuals'.

There is a general belief in a dominant history-writing tradition that early mystic records did not refer to a single case of conversion. For S.A.A. Rizvi the main instruments of proselytization were *qazis* and *mullas*, religious officials in the service of the government. Rizvi notes, like others who argue about 'pluralism' in medieval India, that Mughal emperor Akbar's policy decisions put an end to the political and economic incentives which had previously led Hindus to embrace Islam. As the emperor himself moved away from Islam, he 'totally stopped conversion' by force.

The Sufi texts of medieval and early modern India present the image of the shaikh as the main agent for proselytization and propagation of Islam. The Sufi shaikhs such as Muinuddin Sijzi, Jalaluddin Tabrezi, Fariduddin Ganj-i-Shakar, Qutbuddin Bakhtiyar Kaki, and Saiyid Ashraf Jahangir Simnani are chiefly portrayed as the propagators of Islam in north India. Caste oppression and the drawing capability that egalitarian Islam might have, or for that matter economic and political dimensions, are not mentioned in the literature as factors for conversion. The one recurrent motive for conversion of individuals and at times of the entire locality or town is the attraction to the miracle-working shaikh.

The accounts of conversion are generally the sequel to the outcome of the contests involving the visiting shaikh and a local challenger, or a Yogi visiting the *jama'atkhana* of the shaikh to test his spiritual accomplishments; or the shaikh's thaumaturgic role such as his revival of the dead and protection from malevolent supernatural beings.

There is an interesting story of the miraculous encounter of Muinuddin Sijzi's *pir*, Usman Harwani,[49] after his arrival at a village of fire-worshippers, which points to the growth of such legends. Let us begin with Chiragh-i-Dehli's account in *Khair-ul-Majalis*. It is reported that after his arrival at the village, the shaikh addressed the inhabitants and suggested that since they were worshipping the fire for long, it should not burn anyone who jumped into it. The people were frightened and no one volunteered to do so. The shaikh then asked whether they would convert to Islam if he entered the fire-chamber, sat there for some time and came out unscathed. When they agreed to the proposal, the shaikh immediately took a child of a Hindu (*hindu bachche*) in his arms and plunged into the fire. The Hindus and the fire worshippers who were gathered there recited the *kalima,* profession of faith in Islam, and embraced the religion when the shaikh achieved the feat.

The shaikh, then, came out of the fire-chamber with the child in tow. When the people asked the child how he felt inside, he announced in Hindawi language that it seemed as if he was sitting in a garden (*be-zuban hindawi guft ke man dar miyan-i-bagh nashiste budam*).[50] It might be relevant to point out here that this anecdote appears in an 'authentic' *malfuzat* collection, though such classification of Sufi literature as 'authentic' and 'spurious' need a reconsideration.

A later account shows how successive accounts kept adding to the lore of magic-wielding Sufis. Providing the background of this encounter, Shaikh Jamali narrates that Usman Harwani was actually provoked by the head priest of the mammoth fire temple to resort to this marvellous exploit. Elaborating further, Jamali has recorded that after the conversion of several thousand villagers to Islam, the shaikh accepted the priest, Bakhtiya, as disciple. He was trained in mystic discipline, joined the rank of the saints and became renowned as Shaikh Abdullah. The child was given the name of Ibrahim. He also grew up to be a saint. The fire temple was demolished by the people and in course of time a big shrine complex emerged on the site which also housed the tombs of Abdullah and Ibrahim. Jamali has sought to provide an element of authenticity to his account by informing that he had actually visited the site, stayed there for about a fortnight and received blessings. The locals informed Jamali that Usman Harwani had resided there for two and a half years. His hospice (*khanqah*), including the inner chamber (*hujra*), was intact at the time of Jamali's visit.[51]

Another interesting instance of the growth of the legend of a Sufi is the case of the first Sufi shaikh who settled in Ajmer in the early 13th century. Modern scholars have complained about the paucity of information on the activities of Muinuddin Chishti in the literature of the Delhi Sultanate and suggest that the popular devotion to the shaikh and the legends associated with him emerged only after the decay and decline of the Sultanate from the 16th century onwards. On the contrary, at least three *malfuzat* collections, the *Anis-ul-Arwah, Dalil-ul-Arifin*, and the *Fawa'id-us-Salikin,* which were in circulation in the mid-14th-century Delhi Sultanate, primarily focus on the life and activities of Muinuddin Chishti. Besides, *Asrar-ul-Auliya*, the collection of the *malfuzat* of Fariduddin Ganj-i-Shakar, also contained several anecdotes related to the shaikh. Amir Khwurd has used the material in these *malfuzat* collections for writing biographical accounts of the shaikh and his important disciples. Writing in the early-16th century, Shaikh Jamali has further elaborated the accounts in the light of his own on-the-spot study of Sufi centres and the popular construct of their history.

It will be interesting to turn to the growth of legends involving Muinuddin's arrival at Ajmer, and his 'successful' encounter with the local ruler. We begin with *Dalil-ul-Arifin*, collection of the discourses of the shaikh compiled by Bakhtiyar Kaki. In his compilation, the disciple of Muinuddin and Sufi, Khwaja Bakhtiyar Kaki records that there was not much piety or propagation of the Islamic faith before the shaikh's arrival. When the blessed feet of the shaikh reached the place, there was unbounded promulgation of Islam.[52] Later, he informs the readers that once when he was sitting in the *jamu'atkhana* of Muinuddin Chishti, it was reported that Rai Pithaura (Prithviraj Chauhan), who was alive in those days, used to say that he would be happy to see the departure of the shaikh from his dominion. Hearing this, the shaikh remarked, while in state of meditation (*muraqaba*), that he had handed over Rai Pithaura alive to the Muslims. Soon the army of Shihabuddin Muhammad Ghuri invaded the city, sacked it and seized Rai Pithaura alive. Thus, Bakhtiyar Kaki announced that the Sufi shaikh keeps fire in a cup, that is, he can injure the opponent; he keeps water in another, implying he can show his benevolence as well.[53] Adding more layers and detail to this tale, the disciple of Bakhtiyar Kaki, Fariduddin Ganj-i-Shakar further elaborates that an official of Rai Pithaura visited the shaikh with the intention of becoming his disciple. When the shaikh refused, the official returned to the court of the king and lodged a complaint. The Rajput ruler sent another official to question the shaikh, who replied that the person was not eligible to become his disciple because he was disobedient; was in the service of the king and, thus, bowed to someone other than God; and was going to die as an infidel. When the king came to know of this explanation, he ordered the shaikh's expulsion from the city. On being informed of the royal command, the shaikh smiled and commented that it would be evident in the next three days as to who would leave the place. In the meantime, the army of Muhammad Ghuri invaded Ajmer and Rai Pithaura was captured alive. The person seeking to become a *murid* was drowned to death.[54]

Another version gets recorded in the middle of the 14th century, when Amir Khwurd wrote on the incident narrated by Nizamuddin Auliya, the successor of Bakhtiyar Kaki and Fariduddin. In this version, Amir Khwurd writes that when Muinuddin Chishti reached Ajmer, Rai Pithaura was ruling from there. The king and his officials resented the shaikh's presence in the city, but the latter's eminence and his apparent power to perform miracles prompted them to refrain from taking action against him. A disciple of the shaikh who was in the service of Rai Pithaura began to receive hostile treatment from the ruler for which the shaikh sent a message on his behalf. Rai Pithaura refused to accept the recommendation, indicating his resentment of the shaikh's alleged claims to understand the secrets of the Unseen. When shaikh Muinuddin Chishti, referred to as *badshah-i-islam*, heard this, he prophesied: 'We have seized Pithaura alive and handed him over to the army of Islam' (*pithaura ra zinde giraftim wa dadim be lashkar-i-islam*). About the same time, Muizuddin Sam's army arrived from Ghaznin, and the tale ended as in the earlier versions.[55]

The contemporary separate line of Suhrawardi Sufis undercut the claim of Muinuddin Chishti as the founder of Islam through their version. Suggesting that the shaikh arrived at Ajmer after its conquest by the Turks, the Suhrawardi biographer,

Jamali wrote that when the shaikh became popular in Delhi he left for Ajmer. Although Islam was already established there, yet infidels of the neighbourhood continued to be a source of worry. Husain Mashhadi, who was appointed as the *darogha* of Ajmer by Sultan Qutbuddin Aibak, welcomed the shaikh to the city. Many prominent infidels of the area converted to Islam on account of the charisma of the shaikh. Many others, who did not convert, showed their faith in him by sending a large number of gifts.[56] Later, during the 17th century Abdul Haqq Muahddis Dehlawi[57] and Dara Shukoh[58] depended on *Siyar-ul-Auliya* and *Siyar-ul-Arifin* respectively, for their accounts of the shaikh's establishment of his authority at Ajmer. Other 17th-century *tazkira* writers have added interesting legends in their depictions of the shaikh's life, central to which is his image as the miraculous propagator of Islam.

This image of Muinuddin Chishti was standardized by Amir Khwurd in his *Siyar-ul-Auliya*. He wrote that infidelity and idol worship were widespread in the whole of Hindustan before the arrival of the shaikh. Stone, tree, animal and even cow-dung was worshipped by people. Their hearts were covered in the darkness of infidelity. With the arrival of the shaikh the dark clouds of ignorance gave way to the spiritual light of Islam. He was undoubtedly the *mu'in* (helper) of the faith. The credit for the conversion of the people of this land goes to the shaikh and to those whose further preaching transformed this enemy land (*dar-ul-harb*) into the land of Islam (*dar-ul-islam*).[59] This picture of the shaikh is also reflected in the non-Sufi literature of the period. Referring to the visit to the shaikh's tomb by the reigning Sultan of Delhi, Muhammad bin Tughluq, the writer of *Futuh-us-Salatin* (completed in 1350), Isami refers the shaikh as the 'refuge of the faith'.[60] Thus, we learn from this and other sources that Ajmer had emerged as a major pilgrimage centre of the shrine of Muinuddin Chishti by the middle of the 14th century. One of the sources did note that it continued to draw the people in large numbers in the late-15th and early-16th century. Jamali wrote that many prominent infidels of the region had converted to Islam on account of the *barkat* (blessing) of the shaikh and those who did not, used to send gifts to him. The continued faith of the people was observed in the time of the biographer who found that they visited the tomb every year and offered large sums to the keepers of the shrine.[61]

Simon Digby has noted that the rise to pre-eminence of the Chishti Shaikhs in India from a relatively obscure lineage in Chisht, now in Afghanistan – with their legends, tombs and shrines enjoying excessive influence – may not necessarily be due to the abundance and variety of qualities attributed to the Chishtis and nor due to any great number of devotees in their lifetime. Such an image and following was built over time, the initial impetus for which came from the ascendancy of the Chishti tradition at a time when they could attract the best of the Sultanate intellectuals and propagandists like Amir Khusrau, Amir Hasan and Ziyauddin Barani, who celebrated the charisma of the Chishtis in their writings. Their early testimonies served as models for building and celebrating the singular importance of the Chishti tradition in posterity. However, as the other set of studies have shown which we have reviewed earlier, the social and cultural roles of Sufis and their institutions cannot be dismissed as mere propaganda; Sufis were venerated as living legends and enjoyed widespread following in their lifetime.

The anecdotes of conversion in Sufi literature, both of individuals and in groups, reveal attempts at establishing the authority of the Sufi shaikh. Contrary to the perception of some modern scholars, the anecdotes indicate the keenness of the Chishti shaikhs for conversion. Reports of conversion of non-Muslims because of a public display of miracles further confirmed the Sufi's spiritual superiority and augmented his claim to power and authority. The view that the early Chishti texts do not refer to a single case of conversion needs reconsideration. An extensive work by the Suhrawardi shaikh, Jamali Kamboh, has confirmed that the anecdotes in Sufi literature were considered as valid in the late-15th-century public discourse.[62] Some later works further confirm Jamali's reports.[63] We may conclude that the accounts of conversion in the texts have, historically, been considered as valid in both the Chishti and non-Chishti Sufi circles and in the larger sphere of their followers.

Further, Shaikh Nizamuddin's narration of the tales of conversion, clearly shows that he was not disinterested in proselytization. He did not approve of the use of force, nor did he recognize the importance of persuasion for 'the change of heart' of non-Muslims. The shaikh believed that conversion was possible through the gradual transformation of heart of non-Muslims if put in the company of a pious person, for example, a Sufi shaikh, or through a cataclysmic change of heart made possible by the Sufi shaikh's miraculous power. The shaikh also emphasized that reform within would be the best means for the propagation of the faith.

A more aggressive approach to the Indian environment maybe found in the activities and writings of the Naqshbandi Sufi Shaikh Ahmad Sirhindi in the late-16th and early-17th centuries. However, Yohanan Friedmann has noted that Sirhindi's attitude towards Hindus was context-specific. Also, Sirhindi was not particularly interested in conversion, instead, for him, the honour of Islam demanded the humiliation of the Hindus. The latter should be treated as dogs, and cows should be slaughtered to demonstrate the supremacy of Islam. In general, Sirhindi's main concern was the reform and empowerment of Muslims. By contrast, another leading Naqshbandi Sufi, Shah Waliullah, adopted a more eclectic approach even on questions of saint-worship and Sufi practice of music. As J.M.S. Baljon has shown, Waliullah offered a qualified approval of existing Sufi practices, which was marked by an evolution of his ideas and resultant modifications in his approach.

Thus, to conclude, the introduction revisited some of the representative writings on the perennial debates on what were the different roles the Sufis played in medieval India. As seen above, of particular interest is the question whether they were interested in conversion and Islamization. Sufi traditions have celebrated, since as early as the 14th century, the image of leading Sufi masters as Islamizers in various parts of the subcontinent. The Sufi writings also claim that the Sufi shaikhs facilitated Muslim conquests of the regions and thus contributed to the expansion of Islam in India. Modern scholars have read such assertions in Sufi literature from their diverse vantage points. This has led to contestations on how to make sense of the sources and what plausible conclusions could be arrived at. It is also suggested by some scholars that the Sufis kept themselves away from politics and government of their times for they believed that involvement in politics led to materialism and worldliness which they wanted to avoid. In contrast, a number of other scholars have observed that Sufis, including the 'great' Chishtis of the Sultanate period, did take part in politics. Some of them even visited the reigning Sultans. Others avoided visiting the Sultan's court perhaps because they considered it below their dignity to go to the court and follow its rituals. The Sufis did enjoy authoritative position in society and their significant contribution to the making and shaping of Muslim communities, even if not through direct conversion, but by aiding process of Islamic acculturation which cannot be ignored altogether. Indeed, both Sufi literature and debates among historians reveal that the Sufis played crucial social and political roles in the medieval Indian environment. In this context, anecdotes and stories of miracles narrated in Sufi literature acquire considerable significance. They reveal how Sufism remains a vibrant movement in the past and the present. A selection of such interesting tales from medieval Indian Sufi literature is being presented in the pages to follow.

Bismillah

Reformed sinner (*ta'ib*)

The patron saint of the city of Delhi, Hazrat Nizamuddin, has said that a sincere repenter (*ta'ib*) of sins (*gunah*) is equal to a pious person (*muttaqi*). The latter has, for instance, never ever in his life taken wine (*sharab na-kardeh baashad*) and committed any sin, whereas the former has expressed contrition for the vices (*gunah kardeh baashad o inaabat awardeh*). The Chishti saint mentioned that both are equal according to this tradition of the Prophet that: the sinner who has repented is seen as if he has not committed any sin.

The shaikh further explained that someone who has enjoyed committing sins (*az ma'siyat zauq-ha girafte*) and eventually repents and becomes obedient, he derives much pleasure from his piety as well. It is possible that even a small fragment of the satisfaction derived from devotion to God can burn an entire harvest of transgressions (*mumkin-ast ke yak zarreh az aan raahat ke dar ta'at yaabad, aan zarrah kharman-haai ma'si ra be-sozad*).

Hazrat Nizamuddin, therefore, opened the gates of his hospice for all kinds of sinners to congregate for some light in their life, with those truly repentant receiving lasting peace to their hearts and mind, provided they were sincere in seeking forgiveness and feared the impending day of judgment.

Self-advertisement (*ishtehar*)

There was a saintly person in Nagaur in Rajasthan, named Hamiduddin Suwali. He was once asked how some Sufis are not remembered by anyone after they pass away, whereas the name and renown of some others spread far and wide after their deaths. How do we explain this difference (*in tafaawute ahwaal az kujast*)?

The shaikh explained that those who strive when alive for their own publicity (*ishtehar*), their name and popularity are obliterated after they are gone (*naam o siyate u mundaris mi-shawad*); and those who do not advertise themselves, keeping themselves away from public glare (*khud ra poshideh daashte-ast*), their name and fame spread all over the world (*naam o siyate u dar hame jahan mi-rasad*).

For, in contrast to the fake propositions which eventually fizzle out, virtues of truthful and sincere devotion are revealed by God for a lasting reputation (*mardane khuda khud ra poshideh daashte-and o haq ta'la ishaan ra zaahir gardanideh-ast*).

The choice is ours for the taking, between fake propriety and sincere efforts.

Feeding friends, guests and the poor (*ta'am / langar*)

The guests visiting home, a Sufi *khanqah*, or a *jama'atkhana* (hospice) must be offered something to eat, at least a glass of water if there is nothing else to serve immediately, else it would appear that the visitor had gone to a graveyard to visit the dead, where the dead person cannot serve anything to the visitor.

Therefore, the norm at Hazrat Nizamuddin's hospice for the visitor was: *salam*, *ta'am*, and *kalam*. The visitor would enter saying *salam*, he would be asked to be seated and, without asking, straightaway offered food (*ta'am*), and then would start the conversation (*kalam*).

All these entailed no caste and creed distinctions, no untouchability, no ritual pollution, just pure respect for a fellow human being, friend or guest, no matter what was inside his heart; and, there were provisions for the benefit of the hearts, pure as well as wicked. Feeding the hungry – poor man or stray dog – especially, was considered a meritorious act.

4

Gift a needle, not a knife

Baba Farid (Shaikh Fariduddin Ganj-i-Shakar), a leading Punjabi Chishti Sufi saint and spiritual master (*pir*) of Nizamuddin Auliya, was once gifted a knife by an innocent disciple. Farid advised the disciple that one should not give a knife in gift to anyone; a needle may be a better gift instead. For a knife is used for cutting something, whereas a needle is used for threading, for stitching.

Stitching the heart and mind of people, uniting them in love for God peacefully is central to Sufi mystical practices. By contrast, knives and swords were meant to cut people, divide and conquer them through violence and bloodshed.

Can anyone make the terrorists and the likes understand the virtue of the Sufi way of practising Islam, loving and graceful devotion to the Supreme Being, whatever his name?

5

On friendship and animosity

There were as many as three contemporaries of Nizamuddin Auliya named as Ziya:

First, Ziya Sanai was a *mulla*-type hostile opponent of Hazrat Nizamuddin, just because he was fond of music and justified it as a perfectly valid spiritual exercise, whereas the former considered it as un-Islamic and anti-*sharia* innovation.

Second, Ziya Naqshabi, based in Badaun in Uttar Pradesh, was a prominent Sufi writer from a parallel chain of the Chishtis, through Shaikh Hamiduddin Nagauri, who was a disciple of Muinuddin Chishti Ajmeri. Ziya Naqshabi was neither an antagonist of Nizamuddin, nor a blind follower; he was involved in scholarly enterprise writing such well-known books as *Silk-us-Suluk* and *Tuti-nama*, an Indo-Persian adaptation of ancient Indian tales of *Panchtantra* variety.

Third was Ziya Barani, who later grew into a major historian, political ideologue and theorist through his works such as *Tarikh-i Firuzshahi* and *Fatawa-i Jahandari*. Zia Barani, along with Amir

Khusrau and a host of other poets and intellectuals in the service of the Delhi Sultans, venerated Nizamuddin as a spiritual master par excellence.

Understandably, Nizamuddin's approach to Ziya Sanai was to dismiss him as one of those creatures who tests the limits of one's patience; he would visit the graves of such people three or four days after their death, praying to God, forgiving and forgetting the pain, and getting rid of any feeling of ill-will towards the departed soul, no matter how wicked when around.

Himself coming from Badaun, Nizamuddin maintained a graceful distance towards Ziya Naqshabi, civility as we call it in modern times – not saying anything against and not praising either.

And, with the likes of Ziya Barani and his friends, Nizamuddin would shower all his affection, praying for their success in this world and hereafter, supporting them to the hilt in times of any difficulty and spending some fine moments as friends and fellow-travellers on the Sufi path of love.

Compassion for dogs

A poignant anecdote in Sufi literature on respect and love for dogs is related to Rabia Basri, a first-generation female Sufi par excellence from Iraq, widely known for her public declaration of her mad love for God. Rabia's aggressive condemnation of ritualistic worship, either for attractions of heaven or fear of hell, as well as violating conventional patriarchal norms meant she was destined to go to hell.

However, after her death, she was seen in the dreams of people who were still attached to her and who asked her as to what treatment was meted out to her by God. She was reported to have said that all her idiosyncrasies or sins were forgiven because she used to feed a dog every night.

Sufi-Yogi encounters

Sufi-Yogi encounters comprise some of the most interesting stories of miracles in medieval Sufi literature. Since written from the point of view of the Sufis, these anecdotes try to establish the superiority of Sufi practices, but Yogis are also often given credit for their control over their mind, body, heart as well as the general environment.

By contrast, the deceptively simple Yogic narratives could disarm and dismiss any challenge to their superiority from other spiritual groups, and they could, indeed, subsume any group or community unsure of its distinct identity, through various means – spectacular bodily practices, consumption of what is now described as contraband herbs, and indeed, sexy chats!

One of the most fascinating stories narrated by Nizamuddin Auliya is about his conversation with a visiting Yogi at the hospice of Baba Farid in Punjab, when Nizamuddin was still young and impressionable. The Yogi had lured the Sufi into a discussion on how the character of a child is determined by the timing and day of the sex of her parents!

8

Renunciation

The patron saint of Delhi, Hazrat Nizamuddin, observed that the world was like a shadow; it relentlessly chases you everywhere, but if you start pursuing it, it keeps running away from you. The Sufis, therefore, recommended distance from the world and advised renunciation (*tark-e duniya*). For Hazrat Nizamuddin, *tark-e duniya* did not mean one should wear a *langota* (loin-cloth) and go to live in a jungle to devote oneself in worship.

A greater form of worship is to live in the world, avoiding trappings of power and prestige and devoting oneself to the service of humankind. Service to humanity is, indeed, the best form of worship in Sufi practice, called *tariqat* or simply *tariqa*. Sufis believe, since God has created everything, the best expression of love and devotion for Him is to live in the world, marvel at the beauty of God's creation and serve it without expecting anything in return, except His mercy and approval at the end.

9

Urs and music

Sufis claim they never really die and so their death anniversary, *Urs* which means wedding in Arabic, is celebrated almost as a marriage ceremony. The Sufis thought their death was like going to God in marriage, a culmination of their love for Him.

The love of Sufis for music is well-known and a traditional Indian wedding party (*baraat*) is also nothing without music and '*band-baja*'. Nizamuddin Auliya wrote in his *wasiyat* (will) that music should be played in his funeral procession! From the point of view of the guardians of the *shari'at*, this was heretical. Therefore, on Nizamuddin's death, a close disciple and respected scholar took upon himself the responsibility of not following the Sufi master's will. The burial procession marched in silence as was the usual practice, the defiance of which would have been a great moment in the history of Sufism, of music, and of personal choice – even if provocative and controversial.

Nizamuddin might have retorted: there was nothing un-Islamic in what the *qawwal*s sang, and sometimes their resonant voices did not need instruments to amplify the impact of their singing. For the Chishti saint, *qawwal*s were to be respected as messengers of the Messenger of God. In these days of intolerance and hatred, some commonly held Sufi practices are also under attack, but *qawwal*s continue to sing the song of love, benefitting the spiritually starved who throng Sufi shrines in large numbers.

10

On the recognition of the excellence of knowledge

Once a visiting young scholar told Hazrat Nizamuddin that he had recently completed his education and had started hanging around the Sultan's court, so that he was able to find employment to support himself. Nizamuddin remarked that knowledge is a great thing in itself, but if it becomes the source of livelihood and for which a scholar has to beg from door-to-door, it loses the respect it should command. As a young scholar (*alim*), Nizamuddin himself had looked for work in Delhi before becoming a full-time Sufi, starting with a difficult life in poverty. But then poverty (*faqr*) and complete dependence on the will of God (*tawakkul*) is a matter of pride in Sufi traditions.

Remembering a female Sufi

Bibi Fatima Sam, whose *mazar* is located in a small but conspicuous tomb off Lodi Road in Delhi, was a formidable character and commanded a lot of respect in the Sufi circle of her time during the 13th century.

Her charitable endeavours, reputation as someone who had performed the pilgrimage of hajj in Mecca, and maintained the sanctity of the ritual purification all her life, as well as her ability to dabble in extempore poetry were a source of a lot of popularity. She could definitely ward off the fakes who were pretending love for God while simultaneously seeking pleasures of the body, a contradiction in terms, with a rhetorical composition like this:

hum ishq talab kuni wa hum jaan khwahi
har dow talabi wali muyassar na-shawad!

You seek love, and life as well
Both desires can't be fulfilled!

Enchanted by her personality, Hazrat Nizamuddin who considered mysticism as an act of *mardangi*, commented that when a lion comes out of its den, no one dares ask whether it is male or female!

12

Remaining single

Nizamuddin Auliya and several people in his circle did not marry: by choice as they flaunted their love for God on their green turban – the turban being a symbol of manliness and green believed to be the colour of love; by circumstance as they were too poor to marry, sire children and maintain a decent household; or wanted to lead a life away from the materialistic culture of the time. Since they styled themselves as lovers of God, they were wedded to Him; their death anniversary (*Urs*, literally marriage) is celebrated as achieving union with God.

13

On moderation in eating, speaking and sleeping

The *langar* for the poor and dervishes at Nizamuddin's hospice ranged from *qorma* and roti, with occasional *tahiri* (veg/chicken/meat *pulao*), to paratha, samosa and halwa. The idea was to feed the people to their satisfaction – a meritorious act. Control over bodily demands meant that the Sufi master himself maintained moderation in eating, sleeping and speaking. Less eating or fasting takes care of a lot of diseases, careful speaking is also recommended in most contexts and the secret satisfaction of sacrificing sleep in meditation is not known to everyone.

14

Emphasizing the value of kindness and mercy

Nizamuddin Auliya pointed out that there were three kinds of people. The first set would not harm anyone, but they are of no use to anyone either; such people are like stones. A second set is of helpful ones; they do not harm anyone, and they are better compared to the first. The third set of people is better than the first two: they are not only kind and benevolent, but also do not retaliate in revenge if someone tries to harm them. They tolerate, which is a sign of their nobility and excellent conduct.

15

Hanging upside down (*chilla-i ma'kus*)

One of the most tantalizing practices of medieval Chishti Sufis was an (im)possible *chilla-i ma'kus,* or the inverted *chilla,* hanging oneself upside down and praying for forty nights in a forbidding posture. The paraphernalia required a secluded mosque with no movements in the middle of the night, a well in the courtyard, a mature tree adjacent to the well, a strong rope, and a trustworthy helper, possibly a *mu'azzin,* the caller for the prayer.

Baba Farid, following the command of his Sufi master Qutbuddin Bakhtiyar Kaki (whose *dargah* is in Mehrauli, south Delhi), performed such a *chilla,* praying to God for forty nights in the privacy of a mosque at Uchch, in Sindh: legs tied with a rope and hung from a branch of a tree, with his head looking into the well in the darkness of the night, whatever the science of bio-chemistry might say on this today!

Sufi narratives claim some other Sufis also practiced *chilla-i ma'kus* before Baba Farid was advised to do so. This might certainly have been improvised upon the practices of *urdh-mukhi* sadhus or natha Yogis, standing on their heads with legs pointing to the heavens, as it were, but as is the case with most Muslim practices it was justified as a practice going all the way to the time of the Prophet of Islam, Peace be Upon Him.

Celebrating spiritual connection above formal boundaries of religion

The *dargah* or shrine of Hazrat Nizamuddin Auliya was thronged by people of all faiths already within 25 years of his passing away. In his mid-14th century biography of Hazrat Nizamuddin, Amir Khwurd Kirmani, the author of *Siyar-ul-Auliya*, has mentioned this, and also written in a manner anticipating the later-day pluralistic slogan of Hindu-Muslim-Sikh-Isai...:

musalman-o Hindu-o Tarsa wa gabr
ze khake darat jumla afsar kunand

chu kafur-o sandal az aan khake paak
be-chashm andar aarand wa daair kunand

Muslim, Hindu, Christian and Magi, all of them,
make a crown out of the dust of his threshold

They apply the sacred dust like camphor and sandal
in their eyes and circumambulate the shrine

This must be among the earliest examples of public expression of bringing together people of different faiths. And, no wonder, the *dargah* of Nizamuddin in central Delhi continues to attract both the inveterate criminal-minded people in our midst and the most hapless of the oppressed – seeking blessings and benediction. The keepers of the shrine are also consistently praying for the legitimate aspirations of Muslim, Hindu, Sikh, Christians – for everyone, for all are creations of the beloved God.

Revenge / Reconciliation

Hazrat Nizamuddin Auliya has advised that if there is a difficulty in a relation between two persons with the situation deteriorating from unpleasantness to hostility, it is advisable that one of them cleansed his/her mind and heart of any ill-feeling or sense of revenge. Positive vibes thus created, even if unsaid or unheard, can affect the heart of the other person and feelings of vendetta or retaliation can be transformed into forgiveness and reconciliation or at least tolerance.

In this context, Hazrat Nizamuddin also mentioned that when dervishes fought, they did it with such grace that people wondered how beautiful it would be to see them in love!

Sufi practices and tales such as these can help in resolution of disagreements and clashes at all levels, whether private or personal, differences within families, or community relations in our conflict-ridden times which are creating widespread anxieties.

And, as the devout like to say: God knows best.

For the love of God

Ay aatish-i firaaqat dilha kabab kardeh
Sailaab-i ishṭiyaaqat jaanha kharab kardeh

The fire of separation from you has roasted
the hearts, kabab
And, the overwhelming desire for you has
destroyed many lives, kharab

One of the finest Sufi figures, Rabia Basri was once asked whether she considers the wicked Iblis, the godfather of Satan, as an enemy.

She replied, 'no'.

They asked her, 'why'?

Rabia answered that she was so engrossed in the thought of her friend and beloved, God, that she had no time for any enemies around her.

On the corrupting influence of life in Delhi

Delhi's polluted environment has always had a corrupting influence on its most guarded of residents and visitors. And, even in the field of spiritual leadership, the cut-throat competition meant the survival of the most resourceful. A 13th-century Suhrawardi Sufi, Shaikh Jalaluddin Tabrezi had a tough time in Delhi, including perhaps facing a false charge of adultery, which was considered both a major sin and a crime punishable by death.

Disgusted, he left the city to travel in the direction of eastern India. While leaving, he remarked that at the time he had come to the city he was pure gold, is now reduced to the value of silver, and if he stayed longer he doesn't know what kind of devaluation he might have to suffer. So, he left Delhi and eventually settled down in the country of Bengal, which was around that time known the world over as a veritable heaven on earth with lots of good things in it, later traditions also call it an earthly paradise!

20

On true friendship and sharing

Shaikh Shahi Muye Taab, a saintly figure of 13th-century Badaun in Uttar Pradesh, once went out with friends for a picnic. The friends prepared food, including *khir*, a heady concoction of milk, rice and sugar spiced up with some herbs (not opium in this case for sure!).

When food was placed, Shaikh Shahi pointed out that there has been a misappropriation (*khiyanat*) in the food being served. Perhaps, two of the fellow companions had secretly consumed some of the milk, which was considered a serious act of misdemeanour. When questioned, the two accused submitted that milk was overflowing while boiling and they consumed only that much. What were they expected to do: let the overflowing milk go waste, they asked.

Shahi replied that their consuming milk in that manner was wrong, irrespective of the fact that the milk overflowed while boiling and rejected their explanation. By way of punishment, the two of them withdrew from the group and stood in the sun till they started sweating profusely. Shahi then called for a *hajam*, barber. Asked by the friends, why was he calling for a *hajam*, Shahi said he would like to bleed as much as his friends had sweated.

The condemned friends had to endure the punishment for their act of perfidy, and, in return, the Sufi wanted to suffer because they were friends after all. Thus, justice was done with the commitment of friendship intact!

21

Khwaja Gharib Nawaz

The patron saint of Hindustan, Khwaja Gharib Nawaz Muinuddin Chishti of Ajmer, preached that the best form of prayers included: listening to the grievances of the suffering people; helping the needy; and feeding the hungry. The Khwaja would also say that people with the following three characteristics could legitimately be considered as friends of God: river-like generosity; affection like that of the sun; and modesty and hospitality of earth – occasional thunder underneath notwithstanding! None of them discriminate in what they have to offer.

Not for nothing do people from all walks of life, rising above narrow religio-political boundaries have continued to flock to his dargah for 800 years now, and even in times when there is so much distaste for political violence in the name of Islam.

Complete submission to the will of God

Complete submission to the will of their beloved God helped Sufis combat adversities – social, economic or natural. In a miracle story attributed to the Khwaja as early as the middle of the 14th century, it was reported that a Sultanate official, Malik Ikhtiyaruddin Aibak, went to meet Khwaja Muinuddin Chishti and offered a cash grant, which the Sufi shaikh refused to accept. Malik Ikhtiyaruddin was shocked to see that the Baba was sitting on a carpet, under which a whole canal of gold coins was flowing! He was told to take away his *nazrana* or gift which had no value for the Khwaja.

In the above anecdote, there were several considerations, which were hedged through a miracle, or *karamat*, a typical trope in Sufi practices: first, questions regarding *halal / haram* nature of Ikhtiyaruddin's income; second, medieval *mufti*s and *muhtasib*s, conscience-keepers of the time, were much more ruthless than the modern-day income tax commissioners; third, Sufis took pride in their poverty than being embarrassed by their new-found richness; fourth, the Sufi may not be sure whether his family of several sons would be able to handle this, gracefully. Sufis were, therefore, apprehensive of any offers of land and cash grants from people in power. Chishti Sufis are known to have turned down such offers to steer clear of the political domain, relying on God's munificence instead.

Self-contentment and dependence on God

One of Khwaja Muinuddin Chishti's spiritual successors, Hamiduddin, who had settled down in nearby Nagaur, rejected a huge cash grant from another Sultanate official. Before doing so, Hamiduddin had consulted his wife and the venerable lady confirmed her Sufi-husband's apprehensions by saying they were happy, despite their poverty, which they were able to handle through cultivation of a small portion of land and spinning a few yards of clothes – both were sufficient for their creature comfort.

Sufis were sharply critical of the hypocrisies, especially involving religious rituals. For them, natural calamities like earthquakes and plague and terror-attacks of the kind led by Changez Khan in the 13th century, who by the way was not a Muslim, were punishments sent from above for the wretchedness of the men on earth. In such situations, when people would rush seeking help from Sufis they would be told it was too late to intervene and save them from the disaster. They should run for their lives, praying to God for help, and prayers may not work either for the peoples' intention (*niyat*) was not good and that is why the punishment. Message here is of complete submission to the will of God, who loves His creations unconditionally, and yet He can be brutal in His punishment to those who defy His diktats.

Love and respect for all of God's creations

The widespread veneration of Sufi figures like the Khwaja of Ajmer stems from the fact that they rose above traditional religious rituals and discriminations to speak in the language of love and tolerance for the whole of mankind. As the Sufis would say, everything is from God, whom they considered a friend, and since everything is God's creation, there is an aspect of God in everything – a position articulated in the doctrine of *wahdat-ul-wujud*, or unity of existence. Viewed from this perspective, a little bit of love and respect for all of God's creations can take care of much of the difficulties in the world around us. It is this understanding that has made Sufi traditions relevant, historically and in the present.

25

Pantheon of Sufis in the sacred geography of Islam

Speaking in a critical language for the need for reform within Islam and just a little bit of humanism or compassion, Muinuddin and a series of his successors – Qutbuddin Bakhtiyar Kaki (shrine at Mehrauli, south Delhi), Fariduddin Ganj-i-Shakar, more popularly known as Baba Farid (buried at Pak Patan, Ajodhan, in Punjab, now in Pakistan), Nizamuddin Auliya (Dargah in central Delhi) and Nasiruddin Chiragh Dilli (tomb in south Delhi) – created a whole sacred geography of Islam in the Indian subcontinent, with the successors and disciples of each of these saints spreading and creating a network of popular piety that has stood the test of time for centuries together.

This practice of spiritually-oriented Islam is in sharp contrast to political Islam which thrives on violence and terror, despite the fact that Islam is supposed to be a religion of peace. Sufi saints have shown, through their practice, that this claim of peace with all is not an empty rhetoric, and that is why they continue to attract large numbers of followers breaking boundaries of formal religions and defying rampant communal attitudes and prejudices.

On tolerance and forgiveness

Nizamuddin Auliya has said, as recorded in his book of sayings named *Fawa'id-ul-Fu'ad*, that patience and tolerance are among the virtuous conduct, especially when they are completely free from any feeling of revenge. In this context, he recited a beautiful couplet:

Har ke u khari nehad dar rahe ma az dushmani
Har guli k-az baghe umar-ash beshagufad bi khar baad

If anyone puts thorns on my way out of animosity
Every flower in the garden of his life remain thornless

Through the saying above, the Chishti master explained that if someone puts thorns in your path and you do the same in retaliation, there will be thorns everywhere. The more advisable thing to do is to try to ignore, forgive and forget about it. The adversary will also be eventually compelled to mend his ways; his heart will develop some sense of compassion, and bitterness will give way to tolerance or some respectful indifference.

This was one of the ways in which the Sufis were able to win the hearts of many of their antagonists; the hardcore detractors certainly needed some stronger treatment, but in general the Sufis recommended self-reflexivity, soul-searching.

27

On Eternal love and self-sacrifice: the case of Majnun's failure

Sufi literature has several anecdotes about Majnun's madness in his love for Laila. Indeed, Sufis admired the excruciating pain endured by Majnun and recommended for themselves similar kind of sacrifice and pain in their love for God. In doing so, however, the Sufis thought they were superior to and wiser than Majnun as, according to them, the latter was wasting his time for a perishable this-worldly object of love, whereas they were investing in something eternal, lasting.

The most interesting tale on this is how when Laila passed away, Majnun's well-wishers rushed about in search for him to report the news of her death. When found in a lonely graveyard, lost in thought of his lovely Laila as usual, he was told of the incident, which made Majnun extremely angry with himself: 'What? Laila is dead? Shame on me; why the hell was I wasting my time all this while?'

The Sufis thought they were smarter than

Majnun in their own enchantment for Allah, as they believed that subsumation of their soul in Him will be a matter of lasting bliss (*fana fillah – baqa billah*).

As for elusive Laila, the pretty princess knew the mad fellow was after her and was destroying himself, but she wasn't going to waste her life for him; her feelings may be characterized as detached attachment.

With due apology to doglovers

A 15th-century peripatetic Sufi, Shaikh Ahmad Abdul Haqq, had a female dog as pet during his stay in Rudauli/Awadh. The shaikh invited all the notables of the place for a feast to celebrate the birth of her pups. Next day, when a local Sufi, Shaikh Jamal Gujari, complained on not being invited, Shaikh Ahmad Abdul Haqq responded that only the dogs of the town were called for the feast held by his she-dog!

Sifarish-nama or recommendation letter

Chishti Sufi Shaikh Fariduddin Ganj-i Shakar (Baba Farid) was once approached for a *sifarish* to the mighty Sultan Ghiyasuddin Balban, who was also father-in-law of Baba Farid. Just imagine the power of the *sifarish* for someone from the Sultan's son-in-law!

But Baba Farid was not a run-of-the-mill son-in-law of the likes our politicians have in modern times. So, Farid wrote to Balban:

'The recommendation letter for this person is being routed through the court of God, if his work gets done, God is the true bestower and you will be gratefully thanked for facilitating it, *mashkur*; your inability to deliver would mean God has willed otherwise, and you will be excused, *ma'zur*.'

Apparently, the no-nonsense and ruthless Sultan who had a lot of affection for his children otherwise was so humbled by this short, crisp and direct recommendation that he chose to be a *mashkur*!

30

On the matters of heart and body

A disciple of Qutbuddin Bakhtiyar Kaki, Baba Farid's spiritual master whose shrine is located in Mehrauli in south Delhi, once came to inform him that he had received, in his dream, a message from Prophet Muhammad: Bakhtiyar Kaki used to regularly send him a gift of *durud* (prayer in praise of the Prophet) every night, which had stopped for the past three nights; the Prophet inquired whether things were fine with him.

On hearing this, Bakhtiyar Kaki immediately called the woman he had married three days back, offered her the dower amount (*mehr*) and said good bye to her (*talaq*). The fact was that he was busy with her for three nights and, therefore, could not send his usual gift to the Prophet.

Bakhtiyar Kaki used to recite *durud* for 3000 times before he would hit the bed; his marriage was coming in the way.

Though marriage is a recommended practice

in Islam, Sufis who claimed to be wedded to God tended to remain bachelors. In doing so, they often struggled to control their body; control of the *nafs*, the lower self, is of fundamental concern in Sufi *tariqat*.

Desire for gift or favour

One should not expect or ask for any gift or favour from anyone, but one should not turn down anything that comes without asking for it, even if the benefactor might be Satan!

Irrespective of the credentials of the one who is doing the favour and the legitimacy of the source of the income from which the gift is being offered, the sufficient condition for the moral validity in acceptance of the gift is that the person accepting it had no desire for it at all and there were no strings attached. After all, the entire Sufi economy was supposedly based on unasked for charity.

A more balanced position of the Sufis is that one should give in charity indiscriminately but should be careful in accepting anything in gift or charity, especially when there is a doubt about the benefactor's source of income.

32

Rabia Basri

Of the many stories relating to Rabia Basri, a first-generation female Sufi who was feared and respected for her iconoclasm, is about her madly rushing around with a bucket full of water in one hand and a bucket carrying fire in the other. When people stopped and inquired about her intention, she replied that she was going to set the paradise on fire, and she will also extinguish the hell-fire. She was protesting that people worship God either out of fear of hell or for the rewards of heaven; few worship just for the love of the divine!

Levitatory escape from orthodoxy

Among the stories of miraculous feats of Sufis narrated by Nizamuddin Auliya is the interesting case of a Sufi shaikh called Luqman Sarakhsi. It is related that he failed to perform the Friday prayers and other external observances of *shari'at*. The custodians of Islam (*aimma*) marched to censure him. When informed that religious leaders were coming to dispute his negligence with him, the shaikh asked whether they were riding or on foot. He was told that they were coming riding horses. At that time, the shaikh was sitting on a wall to which he addressed: 'By the command of God, may he be honoured and glorified, start moving'. The wall immediately started moving up in the air! Those who had arrived to interrogate him were astonished to watch the miracle.

Hazrat Nizamuddin's encounter with Sultan Qutbuddin

Once an opponent of Hazrat Nizamuddin Auliya told the Sultan of Delhi, Qutbuddin Mubarak Shah Khalji that the former refused to accept any gifts from him, while those offered by his nobles (*umara* and *sardar*s) were accepted, despite the fact that the valuables presented by them were actually his. The Sultan accepted the suggestion as the truth and ordered his officials to refrain from visiting the shaikh. Spies were stationed to report if any of his officers violated the order and also to investigate how the shaikh ran his public kitchen (*langar*). When the shaikh learnt about this, he asked his servant to increase the quantity of food cooked. Subsequently, when the Sultan inquired how the shaikh's hospice was being run, he was informed that the quantity of food had actually been doubled. The ruler felt apologetic and remarked that he had been misguided, adding that the affairs of shaikh were related to the world of the unseen (*alam-i-ghaib*) and best left as it is.

Hazrat Nizamuddin's historic defence of music

Sufi texts relate the interesting episode of Sultan Ghiyasuddin Tughlaq of Delhi calling an inquest (*mahzar*) in which Shaikh Nizamuddin was summoned and asked to defend the legitimacy of his practice of *sama* or *qawwali*. The shaikh had to appear in person before a large gathering of opponents presided over by the Sultan himself. The case against Nizamuddin was that singing and music were unlawful according to Imam Abu Hanifa, founder of the Sunni-Hanafi school of Islamic jurisprudence which Muslims in north India reportedly followed at the time. Arguments turned on whether traditions related to Prophet Muhammad, regarding listening to songs and recitation of poetry, could be accepted as they were not recognized by the Hanafi school of Muslim law, *shari'at*. Maulana Alamuddin, a grandson of the 13th-century Suhrawardi Sufi of Multan, Shaikh Bahauddin Zakaria, among others also came to participate in the case and offer evidence in defence of the practice of music. Alamuddin had written a treatise on the lawfulness of *sama* and was a much-travelled man. He testified that musical assemblies were organized by Sufis in various parts of the Islamic world without prohibition.

After listening to the evidence for *sama*, the Sultan then complied with Nizamuddin's request not to ban music and, thus, refrained from making a pronouncement on the subject. According to another report, the ruler pronounced *qawwali* lawful for Shaikh Nizamuddin, but not for the deviant mystic groups such as the Qalandars. This was not acceptable to Nizamuddin for whom a lawful matter was lawful for all and cannot be arbitrarily banned. He spoke to Amir Khusrau and other disciples saying that the so-called men of learning, *ulama*, were filled with envy and enmity, opinions of jurists were being preferred to *hadis* (tradition) of the Prophet, and *hadis* used by the Shafi'i school (different from the prominent Hanafi school) to justify the practice of *sama* was being ignored. He cursed: 'How a city where such wickedness flourished was not destroyed by calamity and exile, famine and epidemic?' Sufi circles believe it was because of Nizamuddin's curse that within four years of the event all the *ulama* who participated in the inquest were exiled to Deogiri, renamed Daulatabad by Ghiyasuddin's son and successor, Muhammad bin Tughlaq. The city of Delhi itself was gripped by mortal famine and epidemic. Every word spoken by the blessed tongue of Hazrat Nizamuddin had come to pass.

36

Blind devotion for Hazrat Nizamuddin

Once Sultan Qutbuddin Mubarak Shah Khalji was drunk. He ordered one of his officers, Malik Talbugha Bughda to remove his cap, which was gifted to him by Nizamuddin Auliya. The malik, who was a disciple of the Sufi shaikh, did not obey the command of the Sultan. Enraged, the ruler took out his sword and said: Remove your cap, else your head will be cut-off. The malik replied: You may kill me if you wish, but I will not remove this cap of the shaikh. An astonished Sultan let the malik go.

37

Shaikh Farid's encounter with a Yogi

A Yogi had come from a distant place to the hospice (*jama'atkhana*) of Shaikh Farid. Showing his respect for the shaikh, he bowed his head and prostrated before him, but the aura of the shaikh was such that he could not raise his head. When the shaikh noticed him, he commanded the Yogi to raise his head and inquired how and why he had come to the hospice. Frightened as he was, the Yogi could not utter a word. When the shaikh insisted, the Yogi said meekly: 'Your sight has created such a terror that I cannot open my mouth'. The shaikh informed the followers gathered there that the Yogi had come to challenge him. Once he bowed his head on the ground, he was unable to lift it. If he were not forgiven, he would remain in that state till the Day of Judgement.

The shaikh then turned to the Yogi and asked him of his spiritual attainments. The latter informed that he could fly in the air. The shaikh asked him to fly so that he could also observe it. No sooner than the Yogi went up, the shaikh threw his shoes at him. They hit the Yogi on his head. In every direction that the Yogi moved, the shoes pursued him and kept striking his head. The Yogi immediately descended on the ground, accepted the shaikh's spiritual superiority, embraced Islam, and went on to become a prominent Sufi seeker of God.

A fine conversation between a Sufi and a Yogi

A Yogi came to the hospice of Shaikh Farid. Shaikh Nizamuddin was also present there. He asked the Yogi about the essence of his mystical path. The Yogi answered that, according to his doctrine, the self of the man comprised two regions – spiritual and profane. From the top of the head to the navel was spiritual region, and from the navel to the foot was profane. The Yogi explained that the essence of the doctrine was that while the spiritual part was all truth, purity and ethics, the profane demanded strenuous efforts for self-control and morality. This conversation greatly impressed Shaikh Nizamuddin.

Shaikh Farid discourages gossip about childbirth

The followers gathered at the hospice of Shaikh Farid were once discussing the reasons for birth of children who later became completely non-spiritual. They agreed that the main reason for such a defect was that the people did not know the right time for sexual intercourse. A Yogi who was present there remarked that as each month had either twenty-nine or thirty days, each day had a peculiarity of its own. For example, intercourse on the first day of the month resulted in the birth of a son of a particular quality and intercourse on the second day led to the birth of a child of different qualities. After the Yogi had enumerated the results of each day of the month, Shaikh Nizamuddin committed them to memory, and then repeated them. On hearing this, his preceptor (*pir*), Shaikh Farid advised him to steer clear of such conversation and knowledge as it was of little use to him in the Sufi path to which he was dedicating his life.

40

The Yogis' recognition of Hazrat Nizamuddin's excellence

Sometimes the Yogis came from distant hill-forests to inform a Sufi shaikh that the knowledge of his sainthood was revealed to them while meditating in caves. Muhammad Jamal Qiwam, the author of *Qiwam-ul-Aqa'id* (an anecdotal account of the life of Hazrat Nizamuddin that was compiled within twenty-five years of his death), records the arrival of six Yogis at Nizamuddin's hospice. It is stated that the greatness of the shaikh's spiritual stature was revealed to the Yogis during meditation. They had, therefore, come to pay their tributes. The author went on to say that he had recorded the anecdote so that the reader of the text could know that great men of every religion had faith in the sainthood of the shaikh. They showed it by coming to prostrate before him.

An anecdote on a miracle-show

Many stories recorded in Sufi literature reveal intense competition for power and prestige among Sufi shaikhs and mystics of diverse traditions and lineages. Often symbolic miraculous contests were held to settle the superiority of a mystic. Thus, Shaikh Farid once spoke of a miracle-show in the hospice of Shaikh Auhaduddin Kirmani at Sistan. Kirmani caused the death of the local ruler who had no faith in his spiritual capabilities. Shaikh Farid, participating in the show, took the fellow shaikhs to visit the Ka'ba and brought them back after a while. The wandering dervishes assembled there counted Farid as an accomplished dervish. They, in turn, hid their heads in their robes (*khirqa*s) and disappeared; the robes remained empty!

Miracle as assertion of authority

The conflict for authority and coexistence through mutual legitimacy was a critical feature of relationship between Sufis and mystics of different traditions and lineages, such as between the Chishtis and Suhrawardis in the Delhi Sultanate. The incumbent Sufi of a place never wanted a Sufi of the rival order (*silsila*) to stay in his territory for long. Often, this would lead to them outsmarting the competitor through performance of miracles.

During a visit to Multan, Shaikh Farid was asked by the incumbent Suhrawardi Shaikh Bahauddin Zakaria to perform a miracle. Accepting the challenge, Farid said: 'If I ask the chair on which you are sitting to go up in the air, it will do so.' No sooner than the shaikh had finished the sentence; the chair went up in the air. Zakaria had to strike the chair with his hand to bring it back to the ground. The Suhrawardi Sufi admitted the significance of Farid's achievements, including paranormal power to perform miracles, which was one of the signs of sainthood.

The Sufis avoided any public conflict for power and prestige by recognizing each other's spiritual attainments and areas of control (*wilayat*).

Opposition and forgiveness

It is recorded in *Fawa'id-ul-Fu'ad* that one of the followers complained to Hazrat Nizamuddin that some people keep making adverse comments about the shaikh, which were unbearable. Nizamuddin observed that he had forgiven all his opponents and there was no reason why they should keep showing their animosity. The shaikh advised: 'I forgive those who abuse me. You, too, should forgive them and do not bear any grudges against anyone.'

The shaikh further said: 'There was a certain Chhajju at Indarpat who used to say and think bad about me. Malice for someone is worse than verbal abuse. On the third day after his death, I went to his grave and prayed to God that I have forgiven him for all that he had done to me. He should, therefore, not be punished because of me.'

Curse of a Sufi can cause death

It is related in *Qiwam-ul-Aqa'id* that a disciple had come to the hospice of Hazrat Nizamuddin. After leaving, he went to meet a certain Shams Gajruni at Indarpat, who inquired where was he coming from. The disciple informed: 'Khidmat-i Shaikh'. Gajruni asked: 'Which shaikh?' The disciple replied: 'I had gone to visit Shaikh Nizamuddin.' Gajruni questioned: 'Why do you pay so much attention to him and call him a shaikh?' By then the disciple was sufficiently provoked: 'Why? Is he not a shaikh? If he is a real shaikh, you will die within a week; if not, I will die!'

The disciple then hurried back to Hazrat Nizamuddin and related the matter. The latter exclaimed, 'poor fellow', and recited the Islamic formula to be uttered on hearing the news of the death of a Muslim: *Inna lillahi wa inna ilahi rajiun* (Indeed, to God we belong and to God we shall return). News came within a week that Shams Gajruni had passed away.

This was an exceptional case of the provocation of the *jalal* or the wrathful aspect of a Sufi's personality, otherwise Chishti Sufis followed the advice of their early master in India, Khwaja Muinuddin of Ajmer: 'One should not curse anyone, if someone is hurt that person should pray to God to guide one's enemy towards the right path.' The suggestion was in keeping with the outstanding conduct expected of a dervish: the way of the dervishes was that they were good in their dealings with the good, and good with the bad as well.

Bestowal of kingship on Iltutmish

There are numerous anecdotes in Sufi literature of Delhi Sultanate portraying a Sufi shaikh's ability to confer kingship upon a person of his choice. The reports of bestowal of kingship to the early 13th-century Delhi Sultan Shamsuddin Iltutmish, when he was only a slave-boy, are repeatedly narrated in Sufi literature. Shaikh Jamali relates in his *Siyar-ul-Arifin*, that Iltutmish was purchased by a certain Khwaja Jamaluddin, who took him to Ghazni, Bukhara, and Baghdad in search of a worthy buyer. The future Sultan, who was a fifteen-year-old at that time, passed before the hospice of Shaikh Shahabuddin Suhrawardi and his gaze fell upon the Shaikh. The veteran Shaikh Auhaduddin Kirmani was also present there. The boy entered the hospice, offered whatever money he had with him, and asked the shaikh to pray for him. Shaikh Shahabuddin prayed to God and pronounced: 'I see the light of the Sultanate shining on the face of this person.' Shaikh Auhaduddin added: 'With your blessings, his faith will remain intact during his worldly rule.'

This prediction is widely celebrated in Sufi literature and political chronicles relating to the rule of the early Delhi Sultan Iltutmish. While referring to the Sultan's visit to Badaun and his appreciation of local mangoes, Hazrat Nizamuddin Auliya remarked: 'Iltutmish had met Shaikh Shahabuddin Suhrawardi and Shaikh Auhaduddin Kirmani, probably in Baghdad, and one of them had said to him: "You will be a king!"'

Protection from enemies

The Sufi shaikh's role as the protector of the people is well illustrated in the anecdotes about Mongol attacks which shook the Muslim world for over 100 years during the 13th and 14th centuries. Several reports of miraculous help rendered by Khwaja Qutbuddin Bakhtiyar Kaki when the Mongols had besieged Multan are particularly highlighted in Sufi literature. It is recorded that the ruler of Multan, Nasiruddin Qubacha visited Khwaja Bakhtiyar Kaki, among other Sufis, and sought help when the Mongols had invaded and laid siege to the city. The shaikh gave him a spiritually-treated arrow and asked him to throw it in the direction of the invaders from the terrace of his palace during the night. Qubacha took the arrow and acted as advised by the shaikh. No invader was to be found in the neighbourhood next morning. The miraculous arrow had created a havoc in the enemy camp and the invaders took to their heels!

Having been rescued from the Mongol menace,

Qubacha sought to exploit Bakhtiyar Kaki's miraculous power to check the influence of the incumbent Shaikh Bahauddin Zakaria Suhrawardi by asking the former to stay in Multan and bless the city. Zakaria, however, had already indicated to Bakhtiyar Kaki that he better leave for Delhi. The shaikh, therefore, left Multan announcing that the territory belonged to Zakaria and it would be under his protection forever.

When Sufi intervention does not work

The belief that a Sufi shaikh had the power to influence the destiny of his territory was given impetus through statements that towns and cities would be destroyed if the blessings (*barakat*) of dervishes were stopped. In fact, according to Hazrat Nizamuddin Auliya, a certain Khwaja Karim used to claim that no infidel could capture Delhi so long as his grave existed there. Another anecdote attributes the sack of Khwarazm at the hands of Genghis Khan to the curse of Shaikh Najmuddin Kubra.

On the other hand, the question about how the Mongol hordes overran the Muslim world despite the presence of a large number of dervishes in various cities is also answered through anecdotes such as the one relating to the siege of Nishapur. The administrator of the city approached the much respected Shaikh Fariduddin Attar for help. The shaikh announced that it was too late, have faith in God, and be ready to face His wrath. Thus, the

Mongol attacks were projected as punishment from God and, after a stage, there was nothing the shaikh could do in the matter. Indeed, the Mongols were identified in several traditions as Tartars, that is, 'the fire from hell', sent by God Himself for chastising the sinners!

Healing powers of charms, amulets and relics

For the visitors to Sufi shrines, divine touch, amulets, relics, and blowing or breathing have been important sources of healing. Implicit in it is the belief that supernatural beings (*jinns*) were behind the sickness of a person. Owing to their spiritual knowledge and mystical power, the Sufi shaikhs were capable of dealing with the demons and providing relief to the sick. The Sufi protection of the people and healing brought the Sufi shaikhs immense popularity and silenced their opponents.

Occasionally, the Sufi intervention would not help cure the sick, for God had decided otherwise. While referring to the miraculous healing powers of a relic (hair) of Baba Farid, Hazrat Nizamuddin informed his audience that once a friend Tajuddin Minai came and asked for the relic for his ailing child. The relic was found missing from the place where it was generally kept. When all attempts to trace the relic went in vain, Minai returned home disappointed. His son died soon after. After some time, another person came and asked for the relic. It was found at its usual place. Hazrat Nizamuddin concluded that since the son of his friend was destined to die, the relic had disappeared by itself.

Prevention of natural calamities

Sufi literature records a series of anecdotes of people approaching Sufis for providing relief to them from natural calamities such as drought, famine, epidemic, and others. The shaikhs brought relief to the people invoking their miraculous powers. Drought and epidemics were seen as signs of divine scourge. People were expected to devote themselves in prayers, and interventions of the Sufis also helped.

Once there were no rains in Delhi for some time. The people approached a Sufi shaikh called Nizamuddin Abul Muwaiyyad and asked him to pray for rain. The shaikh prayed: 'Oh God, send rain, else I would not be able to live in this world.' The shaikh's prayer was followed by a heavy downpour, which almost flooded the city. On another occasion, during the mass prayer for rain in open field, Abul Muwaiyyad took out a piece of cloth, looked up in the sky, and waived the cloth in the air. A drizzle started immediately and then it rained cats and dogs! The cloth used by the shaikh was part of his mother's garment, whose piety was invoked to plead for God's mercy, which did the trick. Indeed, Sufis frequently resorted to invoking their mothers' charisma for getting things done when in crisis.

Qawwali for rains

It is recorded in *Khair-ul-Majalis*, conversations of Shaikh Nasiruddin Chiragh Dehli, that once disturbed by drought, the ruler Sultan Iltutmish sent messages to Sufis informing them that his job was to fight battles and it was their responsibility to pray for the fulfilment of the needs of the people. The Sufis were asked to pray for rain. Qazi Hamiduddin Nagauri suggested that a *mahfil-i-sama* or *qawwali* programme be organized. The proceedings of the *sama*, a highly evolved practice of song and music in Sufi circles, coincided with a heavy downpour, so much so that the people were heard saying: 'enough of it!'

In general, the statements of Sufis, that drought and famine were actually punishments from God for the sins committed by the people absolved the rulers of their failure to tackle the problem of natural calamity. On the other hand, the Sultan's announcement that his job was to fight battles for conquests and it was the duty of the Sufis to ensure the well-being of people shows the latter were not expected to keep aloof in times of crisis. The intercession of the Sufis created further grounds for their claims to authority in the society.

Intercession for safe journey

The merchants and Hajj pilgrims were among important visitors to the hospices of Sufis. Before setting out, they visited the Sufi shaikhs and sought their intercession for a safe journey. Various anecdotes reveal different ways in which the Sufis helped the travellers. Muhammad Jamal Qiwam narrates in his *Qiwam-ul-Aqa'id,* an early account of Hazrat Nizamuddin's life and charismatic personality, several anecdotes regarding the miraculous help provided by Nizamuddin to the Hajj pilgrims.

One of the stories is about the experience of an influential Qazi of Goplagir, who has related that he was an opponent of Shaikh Nizamuddin Auliya and would often criticize him. However, an accident during a journey changed his heart. He was once on his way to Mecca. The ship in which he was travelling collided with a rock and capsized; all passengers on board drowned. The Qazi was somehow able to hold onto a wooden splinter of the ship for some time. Then, just when he was about to drown, he called: 'Oh, Shaikh Nizamuddin! please help.'

The Qazi goes on to relate: 'I saw a Sufi emerging and placing his staff before me, said: "Qazi hold it and come out." I caught the other end of the staff and came out. The Sufi immediately disappeared. My denial of the claims of the powers of Sufi shaikhs was replaced by faith in them. I resumed my journey, performed Hajj, returned to Delhi and when I visited Hazrat Nizamuddin at his hospice, I was astonished to see that he was the same person who had saved me from drowning! I prostrated before the shaikh and submitted: "The way you have helped me in this world and took me out of the sea, I request you for your help in the next world as well. Please accept me as a disciple."'

The shaikh exclaimed: 'I have been sitting here, how come I reached there!' The Qazi suggested: 'Oh Khwaja! the Sufis have the ability to transcend the limits of time and space.' His insistence compelled Nizamuddin to accept him as a disciple.

Self-advertising Sufis

Despite known to have acquired paranormal abilities on account of their perceived nearness to God, the Sufis were expected to hide their powers. However, some Sufis had no qualms about advertising their own miraculous powers. Khwaja Shahi Muye Taab of Badaun, for instance, would often claim that if anyone had any problems after his death, they should visit his grave for three days and the issues would be resolved. He would add: 'Visit for the fourth day if the goods were not delivered; if the fourth day's visit also went in vain, you should come on the fifth day and destroy my grave.'

Not all saints were so arrogant. In fact, it was humility, together with miracle-working, that made people venerate the Sufis. Thus, the relation between Sufis and their followers were seen in terms of mutual fidelity and aid. The people venerated a Sufi and, in return, were blessed with his patronage and protection.

53

Baba Farid's popularity

Sultan Nasiruddin Mahmud of Delhi was marching with his army in the vicinity of Uchch and Multan. On the way, the soldiers decided to make a detour to pay their respects to Baba Farid at Ajodhan. When the soldiers flocked to the town, the streets and bazaars were blocked. Since it was not possible for each of the soldiers to personally meet the shaikh, a sleeve of his shirt was hung through the terrace in the lane adjoining the house. The sleeve was soon torn due to an overwhelmed crowd touching and kissing it.

The shaikh then shifted to the mosque and asked his disciples to encircle him in order to save him from the eager public trying to come near. Not satisfied with merely greeting from a distance, an old helper in the army broke through the circle, fell at the shaikh's feet, caught hold of them, kissed them, and exclaimed: 'Shaikh Farid, why do you avoid the public, you should rather thank God for the popularity you enjoy.' The shaikh was moved; he hugged the old man and sought his pardon.

Attack on Chiragh-i-Dehli

It is recorded by Hamid Qalandar, compiler of the discourses of Shaikh Nasiruddin Chiragh-i-Dehli (*Khair-ul-Majalis*), that one day after performing the noon prayer the shaikh went to his private chamber inside his hospice. His personal servant Shaikh Zainuddin Ali, who used to attend to him in his private quarters, was not there at the time. While the shaikh was occupied in meditation, a reckless unclean Qalandar (a deviant mystic later identified as Turabi) entered the room with a dagger and began to stab the shaikh, charging as many as eleven times. Totally absorbed in meditation, the shaikh did not resist.

When some disciples saw blood coming out of the room, they rushed in to see the mad Qalandar attacking the shaikh. They were able to overpower the Qalandar with some efforts, but the grievously injured shaikh did not allow anyone to harm his attacker in any way. As the report of attack on the shaikh went viral, the latter made some senior disciples swear in his presence that no one will be allowed to injure the Qalandar. After this shocking incident, the shaikh lived for three more years.

55

Fantastic feats of a Sufi shaikh

In a conversation of the Chishti shaikh, Nizamuddin Auliya, recorded by his disciple Amir Hasan Sijzi in *Fawa'id-ul-Fu'ad* we are told of the ability of mystics to fly in the air. Making this observation the shaikh told his audience that once a Yogi came to challenge Safiuddin Gazruni at Uchch, started to argue with him, and asked him to demonstrate his ability to fly. The shaikh told the Yogi that since he was the one who was making claims to mystical attainments, he should perform the feat first. The Yogi immediately elevated himself from the ground defying the law of gravity and remained suspended so high in the air that his head touched the roof of the hall in which this encounter was taking place. Thereafter, the Yogi descended straight on the floor and challenged the shaikh to repeat the miracle.

Safiuddin Gazruni raised his head towards the sky and prayed to God that since the others (*begana*) had been blessed with the skill, the same should be bestowed upon him as well. Soon the shaikh found himself flying in all four directions. The Yogi was amazed, prostrated before the shaikh and confessed that his power was limited to performing a straight elevation in the air and returning the same way, and that it was beyond his capacity to take right or left turns. Marvelling at the shaikh's ability to fly in various directions, the Yogi admitted that the shaikh's practices were true (*haqq*) and his false (*batil*).

Miraculous conversion of a Mongol soldier

The *Khair-ul-Majalis,* a compilation of the discourses of Nasiruddin Chiragh-i-Dehli, who was the leading *khalifa* (successor) of Nizamuddin Auliya, records several miracle stories narrated by the shaikh. For instance, while referring to the sack of Ghaznin at the hands of Alauddin Jahansuz, Chiragh-i-Dehli told his audience that an arrogant Mongol soldier was ridiculing the Sufi shaikhs, Junaid and Shibli, in a verbal duel with a Turk. The latter contested that merely by their power of will the shaikhs can, if they so desire, make the fort – the site of the dialogue – move. Even before the Turk had finished the sentence, the wall of the fort started moving (*hunuz turk sukhan tamam nakardeh bud ke hisar rawan shud*). Beholding this miracle, the Mongol soldier fell at the feet of the Turk and embraced the faith.

Conversion of a thief

Fariduddin Ganj-i-Shakar reports that his mother was known for her mystical attainments. Once a thief broke into their house when all the inmates had retired for the night, except for his mother who was engrossed in her prayers. The moment the thief entered the house, he lost his sight. Not knowing how to escape from there, the thief exclaimed that the inmates of that house were like his family members. He went on to say, 'Whoever is there in the house it can be said with certainty that the terror created by his/her very presence has blinded me. Pray for me that my sight is restored. I repent and swear that I will not commit theft for the rest of my life.' On hearing his invocations, the Shaikh's mother prayed for the restoration of his sight. Having got his vision back the thief immediately left the house. His mother kept silent about the incident. Sometime later, the thief returned along with his family, narrated the account of the previous night's encounter and converted to Islam at the hands of the shaikh's mother.

58

Revival of the dead

Shaikh Qutbuddin Bakhtiyar Kaki was once instrumental in the conversion of thousands of infidels after he performed the feat of reviving the dead through his mystic powers. It is recorded that once an old lady came to the shaikh's hospice, complained that her son was unjustly hanged by the king, and pleaded for justice. The lamentation of the old lady shook the shaikh. He rushed to the place where the body of the slain youth was lying. A large crowd, comprising both Hindus and Muslims, was present. The shaikh prayed for the restoration of the youth's life in case the king had killed him unjustly. No sooner had the shaikh finished the prayer than the youth returned to life. This miracle inspired thousands of Hindus to embrace Islam at the hands of the shaikh that day. Glorifying this 'achievement' of his *pir,* Fariduddin Ganj-i-Shakar declared that the mystical attainments of the shaikhs of his order were unparalleled.

59

Miraculous conversion of a Jewish tribe

An anecdote narrated by Fariduddin Ganj-i-Shakar suggested that once Shaikh Sahal Tustari returned to life to perform the ritual of conversion. The bier of the shaikh was being taken to the graveyard. The leader of the Jewish people, along with his tribe came forward and asked that the bier be placed on the ground. When it was done, the Jewish leader stood before the shaikh and pleaded to make him recite the *kalima* so that he could become a Muslim. The shaikh took out his hand from under the shroud, opened his eyes and asked them to recite the *kalima*. The moment they did so, the shaikh withdrew his hand into the shroud and closed his eyes, that is, died again. When asked as to what inspired them to convert, the Jewish leader informed that at the time when the bier of the shaikh was being taken out there was a thunder in the sky, adding that when he looked up he saw the angels descending with platters of divine light and sprinkling it on the bier. Realization thus dawned on the Jewish leader that the religion of Muhammad, too, had such blessed souls.

Recommendations for hiding miracles

Hazrat Nizamuddin Auliya disliked those Sufis who sought to gain popularity by advertising their miraculous powers. He felt that it was obligatory for the *auliya* (friends of God) to downplay their supernatural abilities (*karamat*), even as it was binding upon the *anbiya* (prophets) to display their *mu'ajizat* (miracles). Thus, Nizamuddin Auliya classified miracles as the paranormal feats (*mu'ajizat*) of the prophets who were perfect in their preaching and practice; Sufis on account of their nearness to God were also blessed with *karamat,* which they were expected to hide and yet, sometimes use them for general public weal. This is what made Sufis and their institutions centres of attraction of large sections of people seeking blessings and benediction. Other mystically inclined people such as Yogis could also acquire extraordinary powers (*ma'unat*) to do things not normally possible for human beings. The fourth category of miracles are magical tricks (*istidraj*) used by tricksters out to befool the credulous people and cheat them.

Dichotomy of moral integrity among Muslims

Hazrat Nizamuddin Auliya once conveyed his concern about the dichotomy of the moral integrity (*sidq o diyanat*) of Islam and Muslims through the story of a Jewish person who stayed in the neighbourhood of the famous Sufi Shaikh Bayazid Bustami. When Bayazid passed away, the Jewish person was asked by some people as to why he did not become a Muslim at the hands of the shaikh. The Jewish man retorted as to what kind of Muslim they wanted him to become *(chi musalman shawam),* adding that if Islam was what Bayazid practised he would not be able to attain it and if it were the way the Muslims lived he was ashamed of it (*mara az in Islam aar mi-ayad*).

The above observation, if read together with accounts of conversion, clearly shows that Sufis were not disinterested in proselytization. However, someone like Nizamuddin did not approve of the use of force, nor did he recognize the importance of persuasion for 'the change of heart' of non-Muslims.

The shaikh believed that conversion was possible through gradual transformation of the hearts of non-Muslims if put in the company of a pious person, for example, a Sufi shaikh, or through a cataclysmic change of heart made possible by a Sufi's miraculous power. The shaikh also emphasized that reform within and the cultivation of heart through spiritual exercises would be the best means for the propagation of the faith.

Even animals have a taste for music

The interest of Sufis in music as part of their spiritual exercise and remembrance of God (*zikr*) is well-known. They rhetorically countered their opponents, who said that music was illegitimate (*haram*) in Islam, by remarking that only donkeys have no sense of music. Serious historical text theorizing Sufi practices have argued that even animals can sing and have a taste for good quality sound and music. It is related by Shaikh Ali Hujwiri Data Ganj Bakhsh in his *Kashf-ul-Mahjub* that a good quality voice does not require musical instruments to amplify the effect. He has narrated the story of a Sufi, Ishaq Mosuli singing in a garden where a nightingale could also be heard singing her own song. The nightingale suddenly heard the fine voice of Ishaq Mosuli and began silently listening to him. Eventually, the bird became so engrossed in the soulful singing of the Sufi that she died listening and fell to the ground. Other tales narrated by Data Ganj Bakhsh mention camels, deer and donkeys getting ecstatic on listening to good quality sound, singing or music.

Bibi Fatima Saam of Delhi

Several references to the spiritual excellence of Bibi Fatima Saam of 13th-century Delhi are recorded in Sufi discourses related to Nizamuddin Auliya and his successors in the Chishti order (*silsila*). Shaikh Abdul Haqq Muhaddis brought together some of the details from the life of Bibi Fatima Saam in his *Akhbar-ul-Akhyar,* which is the finest collection of biographies of Indian Sufi figures from the Sultanate period onwards.

Bibi Fatima Saam was like a sister to Shaikh Fariduddin Ganj-i-Shakar and his brother who was based in Delhi, Shaikh Najibuddin Mutawwakil. Nizamuddin Auliya is quoted by Abdul Haqq as saying that for Bibi Fatima Saam feeding the poor was the most meritorious of all the pious activities. According to her, offering a loaf of bread with a glass of water in the name of God would accrue such blessings from the latter that was not possible to elicit even from lakhs of days of fasting and praying.

Bibi Zulaikha's blessings

Hazrat Nizamuddin Auliya used to refer to his mother as a saintly woman who was wholly dedicated in her devotion to God. During their days of penury when there was nothing to cook at home, she would tell the children that they were guests of God, even if she would be pretending to be seen cooking something. For Nizamuddin as a child, the very idea of being a guest of God was a matter of great pleasure and satisfaction.

Later in life whenever Nizamuddin was in trouble, he would visit her grave in south Delhi and seek her blessings as was the case during the struggle with Sultan Qutbuddin Mubarak Shah Khalji, who was continuously harassing him. Though his own close associate Khusrau Khan assassinated the Sultan, Nizamuddin believed he was eliminated due to his mother's curse. He had visited her grave and placed the matter of Sultan's harassment, which needed to be settled or else he would not be able to visit her grave fearing his own death at the hands of the tyrant.

Bibi Auliya and her spiritual dedication

In the section on female saintly personalities in his *Akhbar-ul-Akhyar*, Abdul Haqq Muhaddis has also written a short biographical note on Bibi Auliya of Delhi. The maverick Sultan Muhammad Tughlaq was devoted to her. She was known for enduring the excruciating pain of spiritual exercises which the most accomplished Sufis were known for practicing. According to reports, she would shut herself in the inner chamber (*hujra*) for meditation for forty days. During this period, she would keep forty pieces of cloves with her. When she would come out after completing the forty-day *chilla*, people would notice that she had taken only a few pieces of cloves, the remaining ones would be lying there. Eating very little or not eating at all is a much-recommended act in Sufi discourses. Bibi Auliya had shown it was possible and necessary to overpower hunger.

Eating less as the most recommended practice

Once established as a reputed Sufi figure, Hazrat Nizamuddin spent his life in complete devotion to the Sufi practices of less sleeping, less eating and spending time in prayers, besides meeting followers and visitors – service to the people being an important form of prayer.

During this period, most of the days were spent in fasting. He would take some water at the time of *iftaar* and mostly avoid eating anything at the time of *sahri* in the morning, before resuming fasting again. When reminded by the servant that he had hardly eaten anything at *iftaar* and if he didn't eat anything for *sahri* as well he would become weak and fall ill, Hazrat Nizamuddin would start crying and point out that many poor and indigent people and dervishes can be seen lying empty stomach in mosques and bazaars. How could he eat anything when he is aware of their miserable conditions? Hearing this, the servant would be compelled to remove the food laid out for the shaikh.

The tragedy of Mansur Hallaj and the need for a spiritual guide

Sufi traditions have recommended the need for a spiritual guide, the lack of whom could lead people into trouble. This is the case with Mansur Hallaj. He was looking for a Sufi of his choice for guiding him through the recommended Sufi path.

The founder of the Qadiri *silsila* and much respected in all traditions of Sufis, Shaikh Abdul Qadir Jilani is reported to have said that Mansur Hallaj was an accomplished friend and lover of God. He, however, slipped into publicly revealing his spiritual experiences of the kind that led him to utter that fateful expression of *Ana'l Haqq* (I am God) which led to his public execution by the state. There was no one available to him at that time who could hold his hand and guide him through the slippery stages of Sufism, before the mystic emerged as a reconstructed and evolved personality. Abdul Qadir Jilani added that if he were around in Hallaj's time who was looking around for a spiritual guide, he would have offered to be his preceptor and guide him.

In this context, Hazrat Nizamuddin has also added that it does not matter a Sufi had agreed to guide a disciple or not. More important is that whether a person is seeking guidance from that particular Sufi or not. Thus, if a Sufi shaikh claimed someone to be his disciple (*murid*) and the latter denies it, that person is not a disciple. On the other hand, if a person claims to have faith in a particular Sufi, addressing him as his preceptor (*pir*) and claiming to be his disciple, his claim is valid even if the Sufi refused to accept him as such.

This is significant because a blind and unquestioning *piri-muridi* relationship has often been considered to be the reason for the eventual downfall of Sufism as a vibrant, mystical and intellectual movement in Islam. Here, it is suggested that discipleship rests on *murid* and not on the Sufi shaikh.

Knowledge, intellect and love

Sufi paths have recommended qualities of knowledge, intellect, and love as the three valuable features of a mystic who can go on to be an accomplished shaikh. Together they comprise aspects of grace and beauty (*husn*) which are the Sufi ideals of love and fascination for God's attributes and His fine creations.

Such accomplished Sufis were given spiritually-induced robes which they could wear as trained Sufis and carry forward the traditions of their spiritual masters and the guidance of previous generations. It is often mentioned that the mystic path consisted of as many as 100 stages. The seeker may begin to experience revelations (*kashf*) and miraculous powers (*karamat*) as early as the 17th stage. If the novice became satisfied at that stage of *kashf-o-karamat*, he would not be able to advance to the remaining 83 blissful stages of the mystic path, at the end of which the evolved Sufi would have attained spiritual knowledge (*ma'rifat*), brimming with love for God and all his creations.

Training a disciple: The extraordinary case of Amir Khusrau

It is recorded by Abdul Haqq Muhaddis Dehlawi in his *Akhbar-ul-Akhyar* that Hazrat Nizamuddin often trained his dearest disciple, Amir Khusrau, through letters in which he addressed the latter as Turk-Allah. The Chishti principles and teachings are summed up in a beautiful single sentence of a letter. Nizamuddin has mentioned that besides protecting ones's body as safe and clean, one should steer clear of any activities not recommended in Muslim customary practices (*shari'at*), one should maintain a strict vigil on one's time, value one's life as divine mercy and blessings so that it is not wasted in worthless actions, and if bodily desires appear overpowering they should be channelized towards a heartfelt bliss; Sufi *tariqat* has valued all these as the reliable way towards seeking a blissful end over everything else.

It was due to the effect of a rigorous training in

the mystic path that Amir Khusrau – who belonged to a political elite family of the Delhi Sultanate, whose father was a Turkish noble and mother a Rajput lady – would read seven out of thirty parts of the Qur'an during late night prayers (*tahajjud*). Not surprisingly, Hazrat Nizamuddin liked to inaugurate *mahfil-i-sama* in his hospice with the recitation of the Qur'an in Khusrau's melodious voice. It is related that once the shaikh asked the poet about his activities towards the spiritual cultivation of heart. The latter replied that much of late-night hours is spent in weeping while remembering God. The shaikh liked the answer and remarked that the vibrating effects of that are indeed visible in his conduct and personality.

70

Spiritual transformation of heart rather than direct conversion to Islam

It is recorded in *Fawa'id-ul-Fu'ad* that a disciple arrived in the middle of a discussion in the hospice of Hazrat Nizamuddin, along with a Hindu whom he addressed as his brother. When both were seated, Nizamuddin asked the disciple whether the said brother of his had any interest in Islam. The disciple replied that it was precisely for that very purpose that he had brought him to his feet so that by the blessing of his glance he might become a Muslim. With tears in his eyes the shaikh remarked: 'no matter what you say you cannot change the heart of these people'. Yet it is hoped that through the grace of the company of a devout Muslim he might become one, the shaikh added. After this he narrated the story of the conversion of the king of Iraq who was entrusted by caliph Umar to the company of a pious Muslim. The dethroned king had earlier refused to embrace

Islam even under the threat of execution, but the company of the virtuous Muslim made such an impact on him that he came to Umar and professed his faith in Islam.

71

Shaikh Nasiruddin Chiragh's struggles with Sultan Muhammad Tughlaq

The Sufi traditions claim that Hazrat Nizamuddin Auliya's blessings were behind the bestowal of kingship to Sultan Muhammad Tughlaq. However, Nizamuddin died soon after the Sultan was enthroned, so he could not guide him in a manner that would have made him more sensible and accountable. Instead, the Sultan went berserk with many of his ideas which he wanted to be implemented on an urgent basis. This included the relocation of Delhi's prominent Sufis and other religious leaders to Deogiri, renamed Daulatabad, to provide legitimacy to the Sultan's Deccan conquest and help its consolidation.

This meant that many of Nizamuddin's disciples, including Nasiruddin Chiragh-i-Dehli, running into trouble with the Sultan. Chiragh-i-Dehli refused to leave Delhi amidst all the violence and torture, earning the sobriquet of Chiragh or Lamp that kept burning in Delhi. In an anecdote recorded in *Akhbar-ul-Akhyar* of Abdul Haqq Muhaddis Dehlawi, it is mentioned that Muhammad Tughlaq once sent food in utensils of gold and silver to Chiragh-i-Dehli. His intention was to question the shaikh on refusing to consume the food as rejection and disrespect, and in case he accepted and ate the food he could be interrogated for eating from utensils made of precious metals which was not approved in certain juridical interpretations of Islam.

When the food was brought before the shaikh, he took some gravy from one of the utensils made of gold, put it in his palm, and tasted it. He was, thus, able to evade the evil design of the wicked Sultan to corner and harass him on Islamic legal grounds.

72

Recommending patience in most trying of times

Makhdum Sharfuddin Yahya Maneri was one of the most accomplished Firdausi Sufis of 14th-century Bihar. Firdausis were a branch of the more famous Suhrawardi order (*silsila* or spiritual lineage) of Sufism. Sharfuddin Maneri was particularly famous for his voluminous letters through which he guided his disciples on the mystic path. He had travelled to Delhi to become a disciple of Hazrat Nizamuddin Auliya, but by the time he reached the Sultanate capital the patron saint of the city had already passed away. During the visit to Delhi, Sharfuddin met Shaikh Najibuddin Firdausi who immediately enrolled him in his *silsila*.

Back in Bihar after years of wandering in forests, Sharfuddin spent his life reading, writing and imparting spiritual training to disciples. His letters are particularly significant for understanding of key principles of Sufism, explained through prophetic stories and excellent Persian mystical poetry.

Recommending the need to develop extraordinary levels of patience, Makhdum Saheb, as he is known in posterity, would suggest that learning to endure excruciating hardships in most trying of times was a key practice of the seekers of God. Maintaining silence and peace in violent times is the much-valued quality of a mystic seeking knowledge of God. He should, indeed, appear deaf, dumb and blind; keeping the tongue in control in extremely demanding situations, and endure the times with patience, without a complaint, conducting oneself as if he has not heard anything provocative. Indeed, according to Sharfuddin, there was no alternative to patience and self-restraint for men dedicated to love for God, unlike men devoted to this world, who spent their life complaining or shouting and leave the world crying or weeping.

Punishment for calling out a tyrant Sultan

Shaikh Shahabuddin of Delhi, a disciple of the noted saint Shaikh Fakhruddin Sani, was popularly known as Haqq-go, truth-sayer. The shaikh had earned this title by disagreeing with a *farman* or order of Sultan Muhammad Tughlaq. The ruler had ordered that everyone should address him as the just Sultan (*adil*). Many people submitted to the order and began to address him as *adil*, but the shaikh asserted that he cannot call a *zalim* (tyrant), as *adil*.

Not surprisingly, the brutal Sultan punished him by ordering him to be thrown out from the top of his fort. His *mazar* was built at the same place. A short biographical note on him is included in *Akhbar-ul-Akhyar* of Shaikh Abdul Haqq Muhaddis Dehlawi.

Stop using fatwas to defame and bully each other

Syed Muhammad Gesu-daraz was a prominent disciple of Shaikh Nasiruddin Chiragh. He became popular with the title of Gesu-daraz, which means 'the long haired one'. His long hair had once got stuck with the palanquin of Nasiruddin Chiragh, which he kept carrying and walking for a long distance so that the shaikh was not inconvenienced. When the shaikh learned about it, he was mighty pleased by the extreme attachment and devotion of Gesu-daraz for him. Abdul Haqq Muhaddis writes a couplet, said to have been quoted by Nasiruddin Chiragh on the occasion:

Har ke murid syed gesu-daraz shud
Wallah khilaaf nist ke u ishqbaz shud
Whoever became a disciple of syed gesu-daraz
By God, without doubt, became a connoisseur of love

Gesu-daraz himself was careful about not saying or doing anything that would be considered not recommended in Islamic juridical interpretations. Even on the question of listening to song and music, *sama* (which included soulful song and ecstatic dance), he suggested self-restraint. A learned author of several books, he would enter into theological disputations, displaying scholarly excellence and maintaining integrity.

On the raging debate concerning the difference between Sufis and *ulama* (Muslim religious scholars), Gesu-daraz explained that there is no distinction except that the Sufis sought to annihilate themselves (*fana*) in the person of God so as to forget about their own existence (*wujud*). The *ulama* involved in seeking knowledge should not merely be concerned about Islamic learning on principles of prophetic traditions (*hadis*), jurisprudence (*fiqh*), Qur'anic commentary (*tafsir*), etc. True learning is knowing the person and attributes of God, which is a matter of spiritual experience and not pedagogic arguments only.

Gesu-daraz is, thus, seen here as someone who not only tried to bridge the gulf between Sufis and *ulama*, but also rise above sectarian divisions by criticizing the way Muslims conducted themselves, both in their virtuous self-presentation as pietistic devout and in falsely condemning and attacking others for innovations in their practice of Islam. In sum, from his strong position in both scholarly and mystical traditions, Gesu-daraz was calling Muslims to refrain from hurling *fatwas* to defame each other. No wonder, he commanded a lot of respect in Delhi and had a large following in Gulbarga in Deccan, where he relocated himself before the sacking of Delhi in 1398 by Timur.

Till death do us part and after

Syed Muhammad Gesu-daraz had nominated his grandson Sadidullah as his spiritual successor when he was still a child. Whenever someone would come to become his disciple, Gesu-daraz would pass him on to Sadidullah after some instructions. The latter was known to be deeply devoted to the idea of love for God.

However, Sadidullah fell in love with a woman. For long, he kept his heart in control and the matter a secret. Eventually, he took her in marriage or *nikah*. When they met on the wedding morning, as per the custom, she passed away as soon as he saw her beautiful face. The celebrations of marriage ceremony were turned into a sorrowful affair. A shocked Sadidullah took her hand and before he could sit next to her, he also collapsed and was found dead. The bereaved families buried them next to each other. His was true love for her, whatever may be the reason for her death.

This worldly object of love versus eternal and divine love

It is related that when Shaikh Payare met Syed Muhammad Gesu-daraz to become a disciple, the latter asked him whether he had any experience of falling in love. Blushing, Shaikh Payare submitted with some difficulty that he wanted to become his disciple to learn about love, for he did not know what it was. Gesu-daraz insisted that he wanted to test and know the levels of his emotions concerning matters of love. He should, therefore, frankly narrate any incident relating to love that he may have experienced.

Sufficiently encouraged, Payare opened up to recount that he had once fallen in love with a non-Muslim woman. Since there was no way he could meet her, he wore a sacred thread and went to the temple where she would come for worship so that he could see her to his heart's satisfaction.

On hearing this, Gesu-daraz embraced him and said he would not get a bolder and more determined person around him. The shaikh took him under his guidance to train him into becoming a true lover of God, *ishq-haqiqi*. He was directed to perform forty-day long spiritual exercises, *chilla*, in the room that was known to have been previously acquired by Baba Farid, inside the tomb complex of Shaikh Qutbuddin Bakhtiyar Kaki in Mehrauli, Delhi. He was, thus, deeply sunk in rigorous training through excruciating spiritual exercises and meditation over a long period of time. This made him an accomplished Sufi acquiring an exalted status, known as a formidable *murid* of Gesu-daraz's grandson and successor, Sadidullah.

Political violence and butchering

Most traditions of Sufism have recommended steering clear of political regimes. They maintain a distinction between political and spiritual domains to remove any confusion in the minds of rulers regarding any political ambition, which could be legitimized through their wide popularity. Others maintain a workable relation with political powers, offering to pray for them and providing legitimacy. A third set works in tandem in which religious and political powers get enmeshed with each other. The fourth approach threatens political regimes altogether. One such case culminated in a major political onslaught and orgy of violence related to a Sufi from Gujarat who had settled in Bengal.

Shaikh Jalal Gujarati was an accomplished Sufi master, miracle-worker, and a perfect friend of God. He was trained in Chishti mysticism by Shaikh Payare, who in turn was a disciple of Syed Muhammad Gesu-daraz, a spiritual successor of

Nasiruddin Chiragh-i-Dehli. This connected him to Hazrat Nizamuddin Auliya's large circle of disciples and followers spread across Hindustan, Gujarat, Deccan and Bengal. Shaikh Jalal Gujarati himself had settled down in Bengal, where Chishti excellence was already established by Nizamuddin's disciples, including Shaikh Sirajuddin, better known as Akhi Siraj of Lakhnauti (Gaur, Bengal).

Contrary to the recommended practice of Chishti *silsila*, Bengal Sufism tended to get involved in political conspiracies with lasting consequences, either in the form of meaningful political intervention in the interest of Islam and Muslims or facing brutal assaults and elimination from political rivals. The outstanding recommendation was to maintain low profile in public and avoid involvement in political matters altogether.

Shaikh Jalal lived his life like a king and even issued orders sounding like *farman*s. Some jealous people, rivals and antagonists created doubts in the mind of the Sultan of Bengal and presented him as a formidable political threat. Sufficiently outraged, the Sultan ordered slaughter of Shaikh Jalal with all his close disciples sheltered in his monastery-like large *khanaqah* (hospice).

Accordingly, the executioners and assailants

broke into Shaikh Jalal's *khanaqah* and began to butcher everyone present there. When they attacked and killed any disciple Shaikh Jalal cried: '*ya qahhaar, ya qahhaar*.' When they attacked him with a sword, he attained martyrdom chanting: '*ya rahman, ya rahman*.' As his decapitated body lay on the ground, the head lying apart was heard boldly invoking the name of God: 'Allah, Allah'.

Political regimes, then as now, can be ruthless and brutal in suppressing any rivals, real or imagined. It is to run away from this violence that many chose to devote themselves in search of peace through invocation of a loving God, following the Sufi path, occasional lapses notwithstanding. This heart-wrenching story of the scandal of the state and a tragic episode in an otherwise chequered Chishti history is narrated by Abdul Haqq Muhaddis Dehlawi, author of one of the most authoritative collections of Sufi biographies (*tazkira*s) written in the Mughal period, *Akhbar-ul-Akhyar*. Two of Akbar's *navaratna*s, Faizi and Abu'l Fazl were closely associated with Abdul Haqq as intellectual mentor, and the latter also corrected their poetry and other compositions. On his part, Abdul Haqq devoted his time to writing history and scholarly biographies as well as teaching prophetic traditions as someone who had been taught by the best scholars in the twin city of Hijaz — Mecca and Medina. Unlike his controversial contemporaries such as author and translator Abdul Qadir Badauni and Naqshbandi Sufi Shaikh Ahmad Sirhindi, Abdul Haqq refrained from commenting on contemporary politics to save his soul. He had a peaceful end.

In general, Sufis were not supposed to remain silent in times of tyranny. Texts recommended that they should either fight and achieve martyrdom, or migrate (do *hijrat*), to a safer place to live peacefully and devote time in praying and remembering the merciful God. The Sufi has no choice in this matter either, for the almighty God is supposed to determine what is already destined to happen. And, God knows best.

The tragic assault on Syedi Maula

The concept of *wilayat* or spiritual territory of a Sufi shaikh had a direct influence on the political events and material destiny of the realm. The shaikh's ability to bestow kingship, his role as the protector of the people in times of crisis and as the healer of the sick made him extremely popular. Of note is often the massive following of a shaikh among the courtiers and the soldiers. Thus, the shaikh's indifference towards the rituals of the Sultan's court, his refusal to allow the reigning king to visit his hospice and his encroachment into the power base of the ruler, that is, the nobles and the ordinary soldiers, constituted a threat to the political authority of the realm.

The alleged conspiracy against Jalaluddin Khalji with Syedi Maula or Sidi Muwallih as its figurehead is a case in point. It was nipped in the bud with the brutal killing of the shaikh. From the point of view of the Sufis, however, the treatment meted out to the shaikh had disastrous consequences for the Khaljis.

We are told that a terrible wind blew on the day of the shaikh's execution. This was followed by drought and famine in Delhi and its neighbourhood. Shaikh Abdul Haqq Muhaddis says that the Qalandars of Shaikh Abu Bakr Tusi killed Syedi Maula. The divine retribution in the form of a terrifying wind and dark clouds on the day of the execution forced Jalaluddin Khalji to have faith in the Sufis.

Introspection within Sufi traditions mentions Syedi Maula deviating from the advice in Delhi's Chishti circle of not building monastic *khanaqah*s and also steering clear of matters political. This must have been the suggestion to him also during his brief association with Baba Farid. Having extraordinary miraculous power or listening to music would not have been enough to charge Syedi Maula of anything demanding murderous assault, but suspicion or accusation of political ambition and association with courtiers and nobles of suspected credentials turned out to be a fatally-flawed conduct.

Legitimate form of Sufi music

According to Amir Khwurd, the 14th-century author of *Siyar-ul-Auliya,* Hazrat Nizamuddin Auliya identified four kinds of musical practice: *halal* (lawful), *haram* (forbidden), *makruh* (abominable) and *mubah* (permissible). If the connoisseur *(sahib-i wajd o haal)* is fairly attracted towards the divine, then his practice of *sama* is *mubah;* if he is inclined more towards *majaz* (this-worldly concerns), then it is *makruh;* if his interest is entirely for *majaz,* then it is *haram;* and if he is fully devoted to God, *sama* is *halal* for him. The practitioner of music (*sahib-i sama)* should be capable of understanding these distinctions.

Amir Khwurd further writes, quoting from Nizamuddin's remarks (recorded in *Fawa'id-ul-Fu'ad),* that the singer *(musma)* should be an adult male, and not a boy or woman. The heart of the listener (*mustame)* should be full of love and devotion for God. The content (*masmu)* should not be vulgar *(fahash, hazal)*. Musical instruments *(ala-i sama)* such as *Chang* and *Rabab* should not be used in *majlis-i-sama*. Nizamuddin emphasized during his conversations with disciples that whatever was being heard was for remembering God *(yaad-i-haqq)* and, thus, a valid *(halal)* act.

Nizamuddin is also reported to have outlined the *adab* or norms for *sama*: it should be held at an appropriate time when the heart is free from any anxiety; it should be organized at a place where the environment is soul-refreshing; the participants should belong to the same group of male adults known for their addiction *(zauq)* for *sama,* which in practice was a blend of poetry, music and dance. At the time of settling down in the *majlis* (musical assembly), one should wear a neat and perfumed attire.

Maulana Fakhruddin Zarradi's defence of music

Maulana Fakhruddin Zarradi, a *khalifa* (one of the spiritual successors) of Nizamuddin Auliya actively participated in the discussion on the legitimacy of Sufi music. According to Zarradi, *sama* should be listened to with full attention. The participants of the *majlis* should not look at each other or be conscious of each other's presence. Clearing one's throat and yawning should be avoided. The heads should be lowered and completely lost in contemplation. There should not be any movement of the body and one should keep one's *nafs* (the sensual aspect of one's being) in control so that dancing and clapping are avoided.

However, if one is so lost or moved while listening to music that one suddenly starts crying, shaking or dancing, and his intention is not marred by any sense of ostentation or hypocrisy, then his actions will be treated as *mubah* (permissible). For, crying and wailing to drown one's sorrows *(gham),* and dancing is equivalent to *surur* (cheerfulness, exhilaration) which is a valid movement or activity. Among the recommended norms in *adab-i-sama* is included the suggestion that if a fellow participant stands up in *wajd,* moved or transported in an ecstasy of love for God, then others in the *majlis* should follow him in standing up to be by his side. And, while dancing in ecstasy *(raqs),* he should maintain a certain degree of grace so that others do not consider his movements and intention as vulgar or are put off by them.

All this was explained during the raging debate on legitimacy of music which was being used to harass Nizamuddin Auliya during the reign of Sultan Ghiyasuddin Tughlaq, an incident mentioned earlier in the book. After both Hazrat Nizamuddin and Ghiyasuddin Tughlaq had passed away, the new Sultan Muhammad Tughlaq persecuted Nizamuddin's disciples. It is related that Fakhruddin Zarradi was similarly harassed and forced to migrate to Daulatabad, from where he may have possibly escaped to Mecca for Hajj.

A story of conversion

It is related by Nasiruddin Chiragh of Delhi that after his arrival at a village of fire-worshippers, Shaikh Usman Harwani, the preceptor of Muinuddin Chishti, addressed the inhabitants and suggested that since they were worshipping the fire for long, it should not burn anyone who jumped into it. The people were frightened, and no one volunteered to do so. The shaikh then asked whether they would convert to Islam if he entered the fire-chamber, sat there for some time and came out unscathed. When they agreed to the proposal, the shaikh immediately took a child in his arms and plunged into the fire. The shaikh, then, came out of the fire-chamber with the child in tow. When people asked the child how he felt inside, he announced that it seemed as if he was sitting in a garden. The fire-worshippers who were gathered there recited the *kalima* and embraced Islam when the shaikh achieved the feat.

Providing the background of this encounter, Shaikh Jamali has added in his *Siyar-ul-Arifin* that Usman Harwani was actually provoked by the head priest of the mammoth fire temple to resort to this marvellous exploit. Elaborating further, Jamali has recorded that after the conversion of several thousand villagers to Islam, the shaikh accepted the priest, Bakhtiya, as a disciple. He was trained in mystic discipline, joined the rank of the saints, and became renowned as Shaikh Abdullah. The child was given the name of Ibrahim. He also grew up to be a saint. The fire temple was demolished by the people and in course of time a big Dargah complex emerged on the site which also housed the tombs of Abdullah and Ibrahim. Jamali has sought to provide an element of authenticity to his account by informing that he had actually visited the site, stayed there for about a fortnight and received blessings. The locals informed Jamali that Usman Harwani had resided there for two-and-a-half years. His hospice *(khanaqah),* including the inner chamber (*hujra*), was intact at the time of Jamali's visit.

On the blessed company of virtuous friends

Sufis have always recommended companionship of virtuous friends, identified as *yaraan*. Pietistic friends belonging to the same spiritual discipline such as followers of the same religious teacher can be treated as fellow brothers, *pir bhai*. Relationships between them can be more rewarding than with kins related by blood, because the latter can go astray.

Elaborating on this, Nizamuddin Auliya has further explained, quoting the Qur'an, that on the day of judgement, *qayamat,* some friends will turn out to be enemies of each other, except the pietistic ones. Friends who were close to each other on the basis of their participation in sinful acts will be exposed as enemies of each other. The shaikh recited this couplet to stress on this observation further:

Tura dushmanaan-and in dustaan
Ke yaar-and dar baadeh o bustaan

These friends are your enemies
These are companions of wine and garden

Arrival of Muinuddin Chishti at Ajmer

In his mid-14th-century hagiography, *Siyar-ul-Auliya*, Amir Khwurd wrote on the authority of Nizamuddin Auliya that when Muinuddin Sijzi reached Ajmer, Rai Pithaura (Prithviraj Chauhan) was ruling from there. Rai Pithaura and his high officials resented the shaikh's presence in their city, but the latter's eminence and his apparent power to perform miracles, prompted them to refrain from taking action against him. A disciple of the shaikh who was in the service of Rai Pithaura began to receive hostile treatment from the king for which the shaikh sent a message on his behalf to the king. Rai Pithaura refused to accept the recommendation, indicating his resentment of the shaikh's alleged claims to understand the secrets of the Unseen. When the shaikh (referred to as, *badshah-i-islam)* heard this, he prophesied: 'We have seized Pithaura alive and handed him over to the army of Islam'. About the same time, Muizuddin

Sam's army invaded the city, sacked it and seized Rai Pithaura alive.

Amir Khwurd further wrote that infidelity and idol worship were widespread in the whole of Hindustan before the arrival of Muinuddin Chishti. Stone, tree, animal and even cowdung was worshipped by the people. Their hearts were sealed in the darkness of infidelity. With the arrival of the Shaikh the dark clouds of ignorance gave way to the spiritual light of Islam. He was undoubtedly the *mu'in* (helper) of the faith. The credit for the conversion of the people of this land goes to the shaikh and to those whose further preaching transformed it into the land of Islam.

Conflict between Nizamuddin Auliya and Qutbuddin Mubarak Shah

In his *Siyar-ul-Arifin,* Shaikh Jamali has provided an important clue to the source of tension between Hazrat Nizamuddin Auliya and Sultan Qutbuddin Mubarak Shah Khalji. He notes that after the death of Alauddin Khalji, Qutbuddin had killed the heir apparent Khizr Khan, who was a disciple of Nizamuddin Auliya and captured the throne. As he saw that the entire army and most of the *amir*s (nobles) were disciples and followers of the shaikh, he doubted the latter's intentions. He, therefore, inquired from a close confidant, Qazi Muhammad Ghaznawi, about the shaikh's source of income. The Qazi, who had no faith in the shaikh, remarked that his expenses were met with the *nazar* (gifts) presented by the nobles. The Sultan ordered that strict action be taken against the officials who visited the saint and offered any gift to him. When Nizamuddin Auliya heard this, he asked his servant to double the expenses of the hospice. He also instructed his servant to take the required coins from a cupboard in the hospice by uttering *bismillah* (that is, in the name of Allah, an expression frequently used by Muslims before commencing something). As the news of the miraculous production of coins spread, the Sultan was astounded.

Jamali further writes that later the Sultan sent a messenger to Nizamuddin Auliya and informed him that Sufi Shaikh Ruknuddin Suhrawardi was arriving from Multan to visit the court. The shaikh was asked to be present on the occasion. Nizamuddin Auliya turned down the ruler's invitation. He also sent a message to the Suhrawardi Shaikh, Ziyauddin Rumi, the *pir* of the Sultan, asking him to prevent his disciple from picking a fight with the dervishes. Ziyauddin was on his deathbed at the time, so he could not do anything in the matter. He died soon after. The ruler and the religious leaders of the city assembled at his grave for a memorial service. When Nizamuddin Auliya reached there everybody rushed to show him respect. Sultan Qutbuddin was jealously watching all this from a distance. Some prominent participants advised the shaikh to greet the king. The shaikh politely refused suggesting that the Sultan was reciting the Qur'an and it was not proper to disturb him at that time. Returning to the palace, the ruler called a *mahzar* (summons to appear in the court) and asked the *ulama* to convince the saint of the necessity of visiting him once in a week or at least on the first of every month.

Soon a delegation of the leading religious leaders of the capital met Nizamuddin Auliya and conveyed to him the Sultan's message. They pleaded that the shaikh should visit the court so that a conflict with the young ruler could be avoided. The saint gave a vague reply. Seeking to pacify the king, they informed him that the shaikh had agreed to come. Towards the end of the month, two court officials who were also disciples of the shaikh came to inquire whether he had actually decided to visit the court. The shaikh answered in the negative. Thinking that the refusal to obey the Sultan's order could provoke a *fitna* (disturbance) in the city, the disciples suggested that the saint should invoke his preceptor, Fariduddin Ganj-i-Shakar, for help in the matter. The shaikh responded by saying that he was ashamed of turning to his spiritual master for such a petty issue and added that the defeat of the Sultan was imminent. The shaikh was assured of his victory as he had dreamt the previous night that he was sitting on a high platform facing the *qibla,* that is, the direction of the *Ka'ba* at Mecca in Arabia. In the meantime, an enraged ox appeared and tried to attack him with its sharp-edged horns. He immediately got up, caught the ox by the horns and brought it down. The ox died that very moment. As it turned out, on the fateful day Khusrau Khan attacked the ruler with the help of a few supporters and killed him, with which also ended the rule of the Khalji dynasty of Delhi Sultans.

85

Nizamuddin's encounter with Ghiyasuddin Tughlaq

Shaikh Jamali has related in his *Siyar-ul-Auliya* that after the murder of Sultan Qutbuddin Mubarak Shah Khalji, the usurper Khusrau Khan had distributed large sums to dervishes in Delhi. Three Sufis of note refused these offerings, but Hazrat Nizamuddin took the five lakh tankas which were sent to him and distributed the amount among the Faqirs and the deserving poor and other needy people in the city. Other shaikhs who had received such money from Khusrau Khan kept it in trust.

Four months later, when Ghiyasuddin Tughlaq defeated Khusrau Khan and ascended the throne, he sought to recover the donations which had led to the depletion of the treasury. Shaikh Nizamuddin replied that the sum he had received was from the public treasury, and he had, therefore, distributed it to the deserving, spending nothing on himself. The Sultan was silenced by this response, but his heart turned against the shaikh.

The controversy over the legality of Sufi music, *sama*, came in handy for the Sultan to call an inquest, *mahżar*, in which the shaikh was asked to prove its legitimacy. The proceeding came to an end with the Sultan expressing his regret for summoning the shaikh. No sooner than Nizamuddin reached his house at Ghiyaspur, the news arrived that the Sultan was much ashamed and dismissed his minister who was instrumental in calling the inquest. The minister died soon after. Other opponents who appeared at the inquest were packed to Daulatabad by the next Sultan, Muhammad Tughlaq. The city itself witnessed mortal famine and epidemic for several years. Sufi circles attributed all these to the curse of Hazrat Nizamuddin who had been forced to visit the Sultan's court to establish the validity of his practice of Sufi music.

Qutbuddin Bakhtiyar Kaki's love for music

Khwaja Qutbuddin Bakhtiyar Kaki, a music afficionado and second in a chain of five great Chishti Sufis who flourished in the Delhi Sultanate in the 13th and 14th centuries, died in 1235, after bouts of ecstasy caused by this couplet recited by a *qawwal* in a *mahfil-i-sama* (music assembly) organized by the Khwaja himself:

Kushtagan-i khanjar-i taslim ra
Har zaman as ghayb jaan-i digar ast

The victims of the dagger of submission
Get a new life from the unseen every moment.

Chishti writings recount that the Khwaja was in rapture over three days, and every time he regained consciousness, he would ask the *qawwal* to recite the same couplet. Eventually, the Khwaja breathed his last in that state of bliss, ascending to the heaven in anticipation of achieving union with his beloved

Allah. He was buried at a site selected by him in advance and the shrine soon became a major centre of pilgrimage and continues to be till today. This was a perfect finale to a Muslim mystic's career devoted to God, marked by night-long prayers and meditation; a refined taste for poetry and music; an informed understanding of the classical traditions of Islam; and an occasional performance of miracles either as an expression of benevolence towards the faithful or to silence antagonists, especially the Sunni Hanafi theologians, *ulama,* of the Delhi Sultanate who sought to censor the ways of the Sufis. It was no coincidence that the five great Chishti masters and later upholders of Chishti traditions shared the love of poetry and music as central to their spiritual activities.

Kings' devotion towards the Sufis

The badshah and the courtiers visited the Sufis' hospice, sought blessings from Sufis and received gifts from the them which were treated as *tabarruk* (sacred relic). Shaikh Jamali extensively describes the visit of Sultan Bahlul Lodi to his *pir,* Samauddin. The shaikh, a disciple of shaikh Sadruddin Multani, alias Raju Qattal, had left his homeland of Multan on the eve of Timur's invasion, and travelled to Jaunpur. Then the shaikh travelled extensively in central India before settling down in Delhi where he died in 1503-4 and was buried near Hauz-i-Shamsi in the vicinity of Khwaja Qutbuddin Bakhtiyar Kaki's tomb. Pious and learned, Samauddin was venerated by the leading Sufis and scholars of the time. His son, Shaikh Nasiruddin Dehlawi was the Shaikh-ul-Islam of Delhi during the reigns of Sikandar Lodi, Ibrahim Lodi and Babur. The elder son Shaikh Abdullah Biyabani (died 1529) was also a leading Sufi of the time. Jamali informs that once Samauddin's lecture on the type of people, including the rulers, who will be deprived of God's blessing, moved Sultan Bahlul Lodi so much that he wept and submitted that despite the sins committed by him his devotion towards the Sufis was gradually increasing. He also hoped that this could lead to his salvation. Seeing the Sultan was cry, other visitors to the hospice also started weeping. Impressed by the honesty and integrity of the Sultan, the shaikh gave his own special prayer-carpet to him. The Sultan respectfully put the prayer-carpet on his head and left the place.

Prayers of a Sufi shaikh yield bumper crops

The Sufis were asked to stay in the dominion and pray for peace and stability, and the durability of the rule of the sovereign, who in turn prayed to God and thanked Him for the blessed presence of the Sufis in his kingdom. Shaikh Muhammad Mallawa (died 1494-95) had come to Delhi during Sikandar Lodi's reign and was popularly known as Misbah-ul-Ashiqin. Initially a disciple of Shaikh Ahmad Rawati, he was later trained by Shaikh Jalal Gujarati. Among his disciples were the paternal grandfather of Abdul Haq Muhaddis Dehlawi (author of *Akhbar-ul-Akhyar*), and his uncles, Shaikh Sa'dullah and Shaikh Rizqullah Mushtaqi (author of the *Waqiat-i-Mushtaqi*). Abdul Haq in an anecdote shows the power of the shaikh's prayer to yield bumper crops. When Sikandar Lodi heard about this miracle of the shaikh, he thanked God for the presence of such saintly persons in his Sultanate.

Prayers at Mehrauli shrine for protection of Delhi

Rizqullah Mushtaqi records in his *Waqiat-i-Mushtaqi* that Sultan Husain Sharqi of Jaunpur came to invade Delhi twice in the mid-15th century, but on both the occasions he was defeated and driven away. On the first occasion, as he reached Delhi and laid siege to it, Sultan Bahlul Lodi stood bare-headed and prayed at the tomb of Khwaja Qutbuddin Bakhtiyar Kaki at Mehrauli throughout the night. Early in the morning a man appeared from the heaven and handed over a staff, asking him to hit the invaders. Bahlul Lodi at once made preparations and attacked Sultan Husain Sharqi. In the battle which ensued Sultan Husain's army was defeated, and he retreated to Jaunpur.

Purchasing *badshahat* of Delhi

Medieval Sufi literature refers to an episode in which the founder of the Lodi kingdom, Bahlul Lodi, purchased the *badshahat* of Delhi from a Sufi of Samana. According to Rizqullah Mushtaqi, once three men came to India in connection with their trade. On their way back, they halted in the town of Samana. All three men Ballu (Bahlul), Firoz Khan and Qutb Khan paid a visit to Syed Abban, who was absorbed in the thought of God, and possessed spiritual power and was known for his saintliness. As they sat down, the shaikh said: 'I sell the throne of Delhi for 2000 tankas. Is anybody willing to purchase it?' Ballu enquired whether the shaikh would accept 1600 tankas as he had only that much with him. When the shaikh gave his assent, he placed the amount before him. Keeping the money with him, the shaikh said: 'You may go now. The *badshahat* of Delhi has now been bestowed on you. These persons will serve you.' As they turned away, Bahlul's companions remarked: 'What did you do? You did not have anything except that amount.' Bahlul responded: 'I have done well. This sum was not sufficient for my entire life. I would have spent it within a short time. If he is a saintly man and his prophesy proves true, I would have entered into a profitable bargain; and if it does not turn out to be true, to do a service to a Syed is an act of piety. In no way have I committed a mistake.' The Sufi's prophecy encouraged Bahlul in later years to dream of acquiring the Sultanate of Delhi, which he did – setting up his Lodi dynasty of Sultans of Delhi in the late-15th and early-16th centuries.

The tragic case of Syed Shah Muhammad Firuzabadi

The tragic case of Syed Shah Muhammad Firuzabadi illustrates the popular veneration of the Syeds and Sufis, and the expectation of a certain degree of integrity in their character from the public. The shaikh had come from Deccan to settle in Delhi. He claimed that he was the last shaikh of the chain of Shaikh Abdul Qadir Jilani of Baghdad and was soon very popular in Delhi. This was the time when Ibrahim Lodi was faced with the danger of Babur's invasion of Hindustan. The Sultan used to visit the Sufi shaikhs for their intercession. He was, however, defeated in the battle. Syed Shah Muhammad stayed for a long time at the fort of Firuzabad during the reign of Babur. His prestige and following remained intact under Humayun. Later, the Afghan ruler Islam Shah was extremely devoted to him. When the nobles and the public saw the Sultan's devotion towards the shaikh, they became his disciples in large numbers. Even some dervish offered their allegiance to him and became his *khalifas* (successors).

Two saintly persons, both Syeds, happened to visit Delhi at this time. One was called Mir Shamsuddin Muhammad. A bachelor, he had travelled all over the world, and was a scholar of wide interests. He kept some books and a couple of servants during his journey. He had stayed for a while at Kabul where he was much venerated by Humayun. The second, Syed Abu Talib, was a handsome young man who had fled from Baghdad under unavoidable circumstances. Shamsuddin and Abu Talib happened to meet each other during the journey, and decided to travel together to Hindustan.

When Syed Shah Muhammad Firuzabadi heard of their arrival in Delhi, he tried to attract them towards him. Shah Muhammad had several daughters and was unable to find suitable matches for them. Even before the arrival of the two Syeds, Shah Muhammad used to say that he was an Arab with relatives in Arabia, and that the marriage of his daughters would not be a problem if some of them came over to Hindustan. The arrival of the Syeds kindled his hopes. He offered them his hospitality. The Syeds stayed with him and were very well served. After several days had passed, Shah

Muhammad sent a proposal to Syed Abu Talib for marriage with his daughter. Abu Talib politely refused the offer explaining that he was a traveller and intended to remain a bachelor. Incidentally, the two Syeds were found murdered in the house of Shah Muhammad. The news of the murder created a flutter in the city. People were shocked and their mourning was reminiscent of the scene of Karbala, as it were. The biers of the two Syeds were taken out in a procession with black flags. The young and the old, men and women who participated in the procession cried inconsolably. Their bodies were transported to the holy city of Medina, where they were buried.

Shah Muhammad was accused of the murder. His disciples and followers turned hostile and wanted action taken against him. The leading nobles, Taj Khan and Shaikh Farid, went to question him. He denied responsibility for the murder and suggested that some thieves might have broken into the house and killed them. The case was referred to the leading Muslim religious scholars, the *ulama*, who were supposed to give their judgement in the light of the shari'at. The prominent *ulama* from Lahore, Delhi, Jaunpur and other places gathered. Shah Muhammad was questioned again. He again denied any involvement in the matter and remarked that they may punish him in whatever way they wanted to, but like a true Syed, he would endure everything. The *ulama* struggled hard to gather evidence of his involvement based on which they could give their judgement. While the case was going on, he was kept in custody and had to bear torture.

An eminent Sufi of the time, Shah Aman Panipati was repeatedly requested by the *ulama*, who were already hearing the case, to join them and help resolve the matter. The shaikh refused to come saying that grieved as he was to hear of the murders, he could not believe that Shah Muhammad, a Syed, could resort to such a dastardly act. Further, his participation in a case in which a Syed was being insulted would be tantamount to his own disgrace on the day of judgement. Finally, as he was already shattered by the news of the death of the two Syeds, the execution of the third would disintegrate him completely. Shah Muhammad thus, remained in jail, and died there. The anger of the public had not yet subsided. They tied his feet with ropes and dragged the body through the streets of the bazaars, and later buried him outside the fort of Delhi. The shaikh was earlier also suspected of using malevolent *jinn*s, demons, to get things done for himself.

When a Sufi would style himself like a Sultan

Shaikh Abdullah Shattari, who was a descendant of the famous saint, Shaikh Shahabuddin Suhrawardi, maintained a frightening demeanour and used drums to attract people for training in his Shattari order of Sufism. The shaikh would dress like a Sultan and his disciples who accompanied during his long journey would dress like soldiers. Shattari would also sit on a chair on an elevated platform resembling a throne and kept security guards posted outside the house where he would stay during the course of his tour. Abdul Haq Muhaddis has written in his *Akhbar-ul-Akhyar* that when the shaikh was staying at Sarharpur, the leading Chishti shaikh of the place, Shah Da'ud, wanted to meet him. He forcibly broke into the house, kicked the gatekeeper, who had tried to stop him, and entered the premises – trampling on the gate-keeper's chest as he lay on the floor.

A tragic conflict between Sultan Sikandar Lodi and a leading Sufi

Though the rulers and Sufis normally maintained grace in their relationship with each other, the case of Shaikh Haji Abdul Wahhab's relation with Sultan Sikandar Lodi, of Delhi Sultanate, over the matter of the Sultan not keeping beard took an unfortunate turn. Though the Sultan had agreed that as a Muslim king he was supposed to keep a beard, he said that he would do so only if his spiritual mentor, *pir,* insisted on it. After the shaikh left the place, the Sultan commented: 'The shaikh thinks that the people who come to visit him (the shaikh) and kiss his feet, do it owing to his own spiritual power. He does not understand that were I to cause any of my slaves to sit on a litter and order all my nobles to carry it on their shoulders, they would do so.' When Abdul Wahhab came to know of this remark, he cursed the Sultan saying: 'His (Sultan's) comment will stick in his throat.' Rizqullah Mushtaqi has written in his *Waqiat-i-Mushtaqi* that the disease of the throat from which the Sultan finally suffered was caused by the shaikh's curse. The Sultan is reported to have eventually died of this painful throat disease. He was a handsome man, and we do not know whether he had started to grow a beard to fight the Sufi's curse.

A Sufi *diwana* lover of Sultan Sikandar Lodi

The Sufi literature not only highlights the virtuous deeds of the sovereigns, but often praises them for being very handsome or good looking. Rizqullah Mushtaqi has noted in his *Waqiat-i-Mushtaqi* that Prince Nizam, later Sultan Sikandar Lodi, was known for his excellent temperament and remarkable personality. Everyone who possessed a heart and looked upon him, had his heart captivated at the very sight. He was unrivalled in beauty. Mushtaqi has illustrated his point with the story of Shaikh Hasan, the grandson of Shaikh Abu Lala, who had fallen in love with the prince.

One day Prince Nizam was sitting in his private chamber when suddenly Shaikh Hasan entered it. When the prince asked why he had come inside without permission, the shaikh answered: 'Do you not know why have I come inside?' The prince said: 'You think you are fond of me'. The Shaikh replied: 'I have no control in this matter'. The prince ordered him to come near him. When the Shaikh did so, he caught hold of the shaikh's neck, and pulled him near the flame of the stove which was burning near him, and pushed the head towards it. The shaikh himself placed his head on the fire and did not make the slightest movement.

In the meantime, Mubarak Khan Nuhani entered the chamber. The prince told him that the man was Shaikh Hasan. Mubarak Khan remarked: 'O, man! who fearest not God, what are you doing? Neither fire nor water harms these people. You have done harm to yourself. What can you do against them?' The prince said: 'He calls himself my lover'. The Khan suggested: 'You ought to be thankful that you have become the beloved of a saint. If you desire to obtain felicity in this world and the next, you should serve him.' Then he removed the hand of the prince and raised the head of the shaikh from the fire. They found that the shaikh was not hurt at all. The prince ordered the shaikh to be put in chains with his neck, hands and feet tied, and had him locked in a room.

Sometime afterwards, people came from the bazaar and informed the prince that Shaikh Hasan was dancing there. The prince ordered him to be arrested and brought before him. When he was brought, the prince asked him: 'You call yourself my lover. Why did you escape from my prison?' The shaikh answered: 'I did not go on my own. My grandfather Shaikh Abu Lala took me out.' The room where he was imprisoned was found locked when the shaikh was caught dancing in the bazaar. Seeing the miracle, the prince stopped treating Hasan with disrespect.

Conflict of interest between two Sufis

Syed Husain Pai Minari (died 1535-36) had come to Delhi during the reign of Sultan Sikandar Lodi but did not like the king and stayed away from his court. Some noble women had become his followers, so he had no need to worry about his maintenance. He had some differences with Shaikh Jamali, author of *Siyar-ul-Arifin*, who used to ridicule him and accuse him of debauchery. One day, Syed Husain could not control his anger, and cut-off his private parts and sent them to Jamali. Abdul Haq has noted in his *Akhbar-ul-Akhyar* that there were conflicting reports regarding this incident. Some persons denied that this had happened. The truth, according to the author, was that Syed Husain was suffering from dropsy, and was operated on the advice of the doctors.

Conflict between a Sufi and the reigning Sultan Ibrahim Lodi

The author of *Siyar-ul-Arifin,* Shaikh Jamali has written about his uncomfortable position after the death of Sultan Sikandar Lodi. He had written an elegy, *marsiya*, on the death of the Sultan. A particular couplet had already become popular in the lifetime of Jamali:

Aye sulaimane zaman, aah kujai aakhir
Ta kunam peshe tu az fitna-e diwan faryad

O'Solomon of the times, alas! Where are you now?
(Tell me) so that I may place before you an appeal against the intrigues of the diwan.

Jamali has complained that the new Sultan, Ibrahim Lodi's teacher, Farid, was a despicable person. He presented the couplet to the king and told him that Jamali has referred to him and his other Afghan associates as Satan, playing on the word, *diwan* (minister) and *dewan* (plural of *dev*, or demon).

Thus, the ruler of this Afghan dynasty and the other Afghans had become distrustful of Jamali. Jamali himself has written that though nobody had the courage to harm him, his anxiety was natural. Then he saw in a dream that his spiritual master, Shaikh Sadruddin had sent a piece of cloth for him from Multan with the instruction to wrap himself in it. He did so and performed the prayer of thanksgiving. When he woke up, whatever little anxiety he had earlier had disappeared. Also, Sultan Ibrahim's resentment was replaced by affection for Jamali.

Yet, Jamali has lamented Ibrahim Lodi's hostile attitude towards Sikandar Lodi's close associates who were removed from their position. He added that some unworthy and seditious characters had occupied important positions at the court and became the close confidantes of Sultan Ibrahim. After Babur's conquest of Hindustan in 1526, Jamali switched his loyalty towards the Mughals. He joined the circle of Babur's son and successor, Humayun, to whom he has dedicated his book, *Siyar-ul-Arifin*.

When Sufis could miraculously produce gold

Several anecdotes in Sufi literature refer to the production of gold by the Sufis. It is related by Abdul Haq Muhaddis in his *Akhbar-ul-Akhyar* that once Shaikh Ahmad Abdul Haqq of Rudauli in Awadh was sitting inside his room and Shaikh Bakhtiyar, a close disciple, was standing before him. Suddenly Shaikh Ahmad asked Bakhtiyar as to what he could see inside the room. When Bakhtiyar looked around, he saw that the entire room was full of gold. The shaikh asked him to take some of it if he needed. Committed to the mystic path, Bakhtiyar responded that he no longer required it.

Pleased, the shaikh reverted the room to its actual state. Though there was no immediate exigency requiring the performance of this miracle, the shaikh perhaps wanted to test Bakhtiyar's spiritual progress as well as his devotion towards the spiritual master. Incidentally, Bakhtiyar was in the service of a jeweller before giving up his job to become a disciple of Abdul Haq, which may explain Shaikh Ahmad's preference for the gold production motif, in this miracle.

The author of *Akhbar-ul-Akhyar* has recorded another incident of gold production by Syed Jalaluddin Quraishi, a peripatetic dervish who died at the young age of 25 in 1541-42. Quraishi was provoked by a reference to alchemy made in his presence. Alchemy was said to be practised by certain mystics, particularly the Yogis as a device to produce gold. Though some Sufis believed that the production of gold was possible through this method, they were generally sceptical about it. Quraishi's reaction is a case in point. He said that he wanted to spit on alchemy. Abdul Haq Muhaddis has noted that as he said it, his spittle fell on a copper utensil, which was immediately transformed into gold. Abdul Haq had also heard that the house of Shaikh Abul Fath Jaunpuri (died 1454), grandson of Qazi Abdul Muqtadir, was once 'showered with gold'.

Power of converting soil into gold

In a story narrated by Hazrat Nizamuddin Auliya, it is said that Sufi saint Khwaja Fuzail Ayaz had been a dacoit before he turned to the mystic path. Repentant of his misdeeds, he called all those whom he had robbed, sought their forgiveness and returned their belongings. Among them was a Jewish person who refused to forgive the shaikh saying that he would be convinced of his sincerity only if the shaikh produced gold from the ground underneath his feet. The shaikh promptly performed the feat to the satisfaction of the Jewish individual, who thereafter converted to Islam. He then informed the shaikh that it was mentioned in the Jewish scriptures that those whose contrition was accepted by God were blessed with the power of converting soil into gold. He added that by asking the shaikh to do so he only wanted the confirmation that his repentance had been accepted. An earlier version of this anecdote is recorded in an early-13th-century Persian text, Awfi's *Jawama-ul-Hikayat*.

Conversion of a Yogi to Islam

The author of *Akhbar-ul-Akhyar*, Shaikh Abdul Haq Muhaddis Dehlawi has narrated an anecdote regarding conversion of a Jangam Yogi at the hands of Shaikh Abdul Wahhab Muttaqi. It is recorded that Abdul Wahhab has himself related that during his journey he met a Yogi, deeply involved in various mystical exercises, who would display his paranormal abilities. The Yogi had told Abdul Wahhab that he possessed a fort made of gold and would take him there for a visit, if he started meditating with him. His dwelling was also frequented by numerous devotees at all times who brought as gifts a number of things, including cash. He, however, immediately distributed them among the visitors and never kept anything for himself.

During his meetings with the Yogi, Abdul Wahhab would often explain to him some of the features of Islam which he listened to with pleasure. The shaikh also narrated that since the Yogi often referred to the fort of gold, he paid particular attention towards it. Probably the shaikh meant that he himself took the Yogi for a visit to the imagined fort of gold. He, however, found that the Yogi remained puzzled and returned to his own profession of 'Yogi-giri', after parting company from the shaikh. At last, he repented, embraced Islam and became a disciple of the shaikh.

Lovers unite in death

Rizqullah Mushtaqi records that a student reached a place called Bhogaon in the course of his journey. Being thirsty, he went to the well and found a beautiful girl drawing water. He saw her and was captivated by her at the very first sight. Although, the other women offered him water to drink, he insisted on taking it from her hands. Her companions said to the girl: 'He is a traveller. Be kind to him'. On their advice, she agreed to give water to the student who took his hands to his mouth to drink it. The girl poured water upon his hands from her bucket. As he continued to stare at her face, the water fell down and he could not drink. Irritated, the girl drew away the remaining water from her bucket and turned away her face in anger. Again, other girls offered him water but he said: 'I shall take water only from her hands, otherwise not, and I will die'. The girls said to their companion: 'We offer him water but he refuses to accept it; he will accept water from your hands only'. She said: 'If I ask him to jump into the well, will he do it?' No sooner had he heard these words that he leapt into the well, causing an uproar among the girls. They said to her: 'What have you done? You are responsible for his death'. She felt ashamed and also jumped into the well.

The matter was reported to the local administrator, *shiqqdar*, who reached the spot along with the relatives of the girl and others. The nets were drawn into the well and their dead bodies were brought out. They were found holding each other by hand. The relatives of the girl wished to cremate her, but the *shiqqdar* differed from them, saying: 'She has died for the sake of a Musalman. They have been brought out together, therefore, it is not proper for you to cremate her body'.

It was ultimately decided that she should be buried near the grave of the student, and the order of the *shiqqdar* was carried out. At night the relatives of the girl decided to dig out the grave and take out her body for cremation. When they unearthed her grave, they did not find her body. They examined the grave and found a passage between the two graves. A candle was also burning and both the boy and the girl were sitting on a cot. When they saw this, they closed the grave and went away.

101

The naked Faqir

Shaikh Hasan Bodla belonged to an old aristocratic family of Delhi. Since his childhood, he was deeply sunk in devotion to God. As someone lost in the love for God, his ways were completely heretical and his condition akin to a deviant dervish, identified as Qalandar or *majzub*, whose conduct bordered on madness. Very often, Shaikh Hasan would go around naked and his private part, which he had as a man, would never betray any kind of sensation. It would appear like a lump of clay pasted on a wall. Controlling or taming the sexual organ is a major concern in non-conformist mystical traditions, for it is viewed as central to the attachments to this-worldly attractions. Mystics needed to be above sexual desire, which either keeps them tied to the world or becomes a source of disgrace. Indeed, conquering it has been a major obsession in several strands of mystical and religious traditions. Desire for sex and love for God were seen incompatible with each other.

Following complete detachment from the world, money, clothes, or whatever else he would get as gifts, Shaikh Hasan passed them on to the *qawwal*s and others who visited him, not keeping anything for himself. Despite being so other-worldly, Shaikh Hasan attended religious gatherings, spoke to people and engaged in fine conversations. Some doubtful religious scholars, *ulama*, would see in their dream that Shaikh Hasan was in the presence of Prophet Muhammad and serving him, helping in doing ablution. Some others reported that the pilgrims to Mecca would notice him during the annual Hajj rituals, though he was present in Delhi at that time.

After his death, Shaikh Hasan was buried near the grave of Khwas Khan, who was a close and pious associate of the Afghan empire builder, Sher Shah Sur. The latter's son and successor, Salim Shah, had ordered the execution of Khwas Khan, only a few years before the death of Shaikh Hasan. A pious martyr and a devoted lover of God lay buried next to each other.

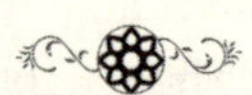

EPILOGUE

Medieval Indian Sufis have generally been portrayed as torchbearers of Hindu-Muslim unity, cultural integration, religious tolerance, and even secularism. Some scholars tend to project the Sufis as deliberately working for the spread of Islam in India, while others criticize them for adopting a passive other-worldly attitude with no interest in the affairs of this world. The opposing views on Sufis and Sufism obviously indicate the diverse questions and approaches with which the scholars have studied the subject. In the foregoing pages, we have presented some fascinating stories and anecdotes, including tales of miracles, which reveal the vibrant nature of Sufism as a spiritual movement within Islam in medieval Indian environment. Sufi shrines and orders continue to exist and draw followers. These stories give us a sense of the differences and similarities of the past with the Sufi influence we see in our surroundings today.

These anecdotes feature in large numbers in Sufi literature in a wide variety of genres, mainly *malfuzat* (discourses of Sufis) and *tazkira*s (biographies or hagiographies of Sufis) compiled in medieval India and many of them continue to be retold in the present. These include the conversations of Nizamuddin Auliya, compiled by Amir Hasan Sijzi in the famous text called the *Fawa'id-ul-Fu'ad*, and discourses of Nasiruddin Chiragh Dehli, compiled by Hamid Qalandar in the well-known text, *Khair-ul-Majalis*. Famous biographical dictionaries of Sufis, including *Qiwam-ul-Aqa'id* of Muhammad Jamal Qiwam, *Siyar-ul-Auliya* of Amir Khwurd Kirmani, *Siyar-ul-Arifin* of Shaikh Jamali Kamboh, and more significantly *Akhbar-ul-Akhyar* of Shaikh Abdul Haq Muhaddis Dehlawi, narrate interesting anecdotes from the lives of a large number of Sufis, some of which have been recounted in the previous pages. In the stories compiled in this volume, insights and episodes have also been drawn from the pioneering eleventh century work of Sufism in the Indian subcontinent, *Kashf-ul-Mahjub* of Ali Hujwiri, known as Data Ganj Bakhsh of Lahore. Political writings of authors such as Ziyauddin Barani's *Tarikh-i-Firuzshahi* and Izzuddin Isami's *Futuh-us-Salatin* also include important episodes relating to Sufism in the Delhi Sultanate. Stories from these important writers have also been included in the book.

The stories of miracles and other anecdotes in Sufi texts frequently relate to a Sufi shaikh flying on a camel-back to Mecca for Hajj, the holy Ka'ba coming over to India for circumambulation around the blessed personality of a Sufi shaikh and his spiritually soaked hospice, walls floating in the air at the command of a Sufi, rivers getting dried up to let the Sufi shaikh cross, a river of molten silver flowing underneath the prayer carpet of the saint, soil, stone, firewood transformed into gold, revival of the dead, many cases of spiritual healing for which the people would crowd hospices and shrines, ability to see distant places and to foresee the good and the evil in future, and the details of the effects of *jalal*, or the curse on the opponents and *jamal*, grace and favour, on those who had faith in him. These anecdotes, with all their spectacular and paranormal contents, can be identified as pertaining to the domain of prediction and divination, encounters with opponents and the competitive nature of popular spirituality, conversion of the opponent and others as disciples with or without direct and immediate acceptance of Islam, and Sufi miracles as benevolence through help in distress and healing practices.

Many of the miraculous stories are recurring, repetitive and common to diverse traditions, and therefore their historicity and truthfulness as historical facts will be difficult to establish. Yet, it is easy to see, from the texts in which they have been included, the relevance, popularity, and contexts in which such stories emerged and spread through the subcontinent. Many of the stories were narrated by none other than Hazrat Nizamuddin Auliya in his own lifetime, and many others were recounted by his disciple and successor in the Chishti *silsila*, Khwaja Nasiruddin Chiragh Dehli. These stories, therefore, cannot be dismissed as unimportant for understanding the relevance of Sufism and its popular appeal. Supernatural feats are indeed the Sufi saints' sources of authority in the public domain. It is only for those miraculous interventions that a large majority of visitors continue to throng Sufi *dargah*s and *mazar*s even in modern times when there is great difficulty in community relations involving Muslims and others. The majority of visitors to shrines are still non-Muslims, for they understand the distinction between the spiritual language of love of Sufis for God and the violent nature of politics in our times, and perhaps also in the past. So while many people visit Nizamuddin Dargah every day, few would be interested in knowing where the Tughlaq Sultan was buried.

In their own lifetime, the emergence of Sufi saints from the seclusion of their hospices to consciously announce their claims to authority in the society or being treated by people as authoritative figures were developments contested by many opponents coming from diverse backgrounds. They included Sufis of rival orders, custodians of Sunni Islam, the *ulama*, the reigning Muslim Sultans and leaders of non-Muslim traditions such as Yogis, Sanyasis and Brahmins. Claims of rivals to authority were settled through miraculous combats with the opponents. Sufi literature celebrates victories of the saints in such encounters. These involved miraculous feats such as sitting in a fire-chamber without being burnt, walking on a flooded river, flying in the air, riding a tiger or a wall, transformation of the contestants into birds, and other forms of levitatory combats.

Notwithstanding the principle of tolerance and forgiveness in Sufi *tariqat* (order), the Sufi saint is often found retaliating with force against his opponent and performing miracles to subdue him. In some cases, opponents die a sudden and painful death on account of the curse of the saint. Alternatively, they realize their mistakes and lesser spiritual stature or capabilities, seek forgiveness, become disciples and get reformed. Anecdotes reveal that the arrival of a Sufi in a non-Muslim locality was perceived as an encroachment in the territorial authority of the local miracle-worker or spiritual power-holder. Sufi literature gives due recognition to the miraculous ability of the Yogis, but ultimately all combats result in the victory of the Sufi shaikhs and prove their superiority against their opponents. Once the spiritual superiority of the Sufi is established, those who had challenged him convert to Islam. Over time, the Yogi becomes a *wali*, or friend of God, and the ruler of a different faith transforms into a pious Muslim *badshah*. The conversion of the Yogi and the ruler is often followed by mass conversion of the local population in the anecdotes. In some cases, as narrated in Sufi texts, the defeated non-Muslim opponents peacefully withdraw to save themselves. Alternatively, the opposition of the opponents leads to their violent end, as in the case of the stories of conflict between Muinuddin Chishti and Prithviraj Chauhan. It is narrated in the Sufi anecdotes that the Chauhan ruler was defeated by the Turks in the second battle of Tarain (1192) because of the curse of Khwaja Gharib Nawaz Ajmeri. Prithviraj Chauhan's refusal to accept the spiritual power and authority of the saint proved fatal for him.

Further, the Sufi shaikh's concept of *wilayat*, or spiritual territory controlled through religious and political categories of authority, was the source of conflict between Sufis and Sultans of Delhi. The Sufi shaikh's power to bestow kingship to a slave, his ability to snatch it from someone who refused to recognize his authority and his large following among the courtiers and soldiers when put together became a matter of concern for the sovereignty of the Sultan. In the conflicts that followed, the Sultan often used the support of the *ulama* and that of the Sufi shaikh of a rival *silsila*, playing the Suhrawardis and against the Chishtis for instance, to check the power and pretensions of the incumbent Sufi shaikh. Among the weapons used by the shaikh in the event of an encounter was also his ability to cause the death of the opponent. Stories of conflict between Shaikh Nizamuddin Auliya and the Delhi Sultans reveal two of them being eliminated from the scene, ostensibly due to his curse. The shaikh's *jalal* or wrath, reportedly affected even the general population as the episode led to terrible famine and epidemic in the Sultanate capital of Delhi. These anecdotes of conflict with the rulers as well as their collaboration by intervening to be king-makers, prayer in absentia for the survival of Sultanate, and other such acts testify to the Sufi shaikh's interest in political matters.

Another set of stories relate to encounters of the Sufis with somewhat heretical mystic Qalandars. The Chishti Sufis of the Delhi Sultanate were sympathetic towards these wandering Muslim mystics, whom historian Ahmet Karamustafa has characterized as God's unruly friends. The abuses and occasional violence of the Qalandars and other related groups were considered a *kaffara* or recompense by the Chishti Sufis, as a sort of compensation for the blind faith of the disciples and widespread devotion of followers. By contrast, the Suhrawardi Sufis of the Sultanate period (13th-14th centuries) disliked the flouting of the standard norms of conduct by the Qalandars. One of the anecdotes recounted in this book, however, seeks to establish that the outright rejection of the Qalandars was not justified, for a true lover of God can be found amongst them as well. Also, a tale involving Hazrat Nizamuddin Auliya to be found in the compilation of the stories here, shows that when attempts to pacify the violent Qalandars failed, the Sufi had to perform a miracle to bring them to their senses.

The anecdotes on the arrival of Yogis and Brahmins further establish the superiority of the Sufi shaikh. Those who came to test the miraculous ability of the shaikh were dazed by his *jalal*. Sometimes, a levitatory contest was also held in which the Yogis are shown to have been defeated. The narratives end with the Yogi either embracing Islam or taking to his heels. Similarly, the stories of encounters with a Sufi shaikh of a different *silsila* portray an intense competition for power and prestige within Sufi fraternities. A possible conflict is often avoided by adhering to mutual respect, regard for legitimacy and recognition of each other's territorial authority in these stories.

The stories relating to the Sufi shaikh's miracles as a source of benevolence (*jamal*) throw further light on an equally fascinating aspect of their personality, contributing to their popularity and establishing their claims to authority. Sufis were approached for curing various kinds of illness, recovery from bodyache and even revival of the dead with the help of charms, amulets and often through 'blowing' and 'touching'. Their intercession was sought for preventing natural calamities and relief from drought, famine and epidemics. They were also asked to pray for protection from enemies such as Mongol invaders and dacoits. Pilgrims and merchants invoked their blessings and benediction for ensuring safe journey. The Sufi narratives show that the people of various towns and cities wanted the Sufi shaikhs to stay in their neighbourhood and protect them in times of crisis.

The departure of a Sufi from a particular area was considered a bad omen – the forerunner of extraordinary misfortune for the area. Nizamuddin Auliya, for instance, believed that the region of Punjab was protected from the Mongol onslaught because of the blessings of Shaikh Fariduddin Ganj-i-Shakar (Baba Farid). In the year when Baba Farid departed from this world, the Mongol hordes invaded and devastated the region. Later, Izzuddin Isami wrote in his *Futuh-us-Salatin* that Delhi was destroyed by Muhammad Tughlaq due to his shifting of the capital to Daulatabad, because God had removed Hazrat Nizamuddin from there. According to him, the rulers were heads of states for only matters political, but it was the overall aura of the mystic Faqirs which averted the calamities in a region. If there were no saints on the face of the earth, the world would not have continued to exist. The world functions by the blessings of the saints. Popularity of a Sufi saint depended upon how successfully he demonstrated his miraculous power. The people appropriated a miracle-working Sufi shaikh, expected him to stay in their neighbourhood and perform miracles for them.

This is a role the Sufis continue to perform even after they pass away, because it is believed that saints never die. Lying in their graves, they continue to look after their disciples and followers. Visitors to their *mazar*s and *dargah*s are thus blessed with the surrounding spirituality and charisma. This has made Sufi shrines relevant for all times, in the past and the present. Spiritually soaked Thursday evenings at the *dargah* and the occasion of annual *Urs* (death anniversary of Sufis) are considered to be especially rewarding. The shrines are open to everyone: man-woman, high-low, rich-poor, Hindu-Muslim, Sikh-Christian. None are discriminated against, for all are creations of God, and Sufis considered themselves as friends and lovers of God. The stories recounted in this book bring out this and several other significant dimensions which together make Sufism a vibrant spiritual movement within Islam, with a history going back twelve centuries and counting. It was part of the great traditions of Islam at their zenith and it is also witness to the contemporary history of Islam at its lowest ebb. In either case, its relevance is a matter of hope and solace for those who seek to live in a world promising peace and harmonious coexistence of all the beautiful creations of God. For, it creates a spiritually imbued brotherhood of unity in diversity.

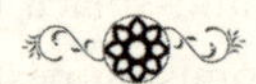

NOTES

Introduction

1. For the most comprehensive and up-to-date historical overview of the early phase of Sufism, see Ahmet T. Karamustafa, *Sufism: The Formative Period*, The New Edinburgh Islamic Survey Series, Edinburgh: Edinburgh University Press, 2007.
2. *Ibid.*, p. 51.
3. *Ibid.*, p. 62.
4. *Ibid.*, p. 175.
5. See William C. Chittick, *Sufism: A Short Introduction*, Oxford: Oneworld Publications, 2007.
6. The term 'orthodoxy' is being used here for the group of *ulama*, often referred to as the *ulama-i-su*, or worldly *ulama*, who insisted on implementing the Sunni Hanafite interpretation of Islam in Muslim public life and sought to use political power for the purpose.
7. For a 14th-century reference to the Sufi practice of *chilla-i-makus*, see Amir Khwurd, *Siyar-ul-Auliya*, Islamabad: Markaz Tahqiqat-i-Farsi Iran wa Pakistan, 1978.
8. Literature on Sufi cults produced on this line is numerous,

but see, K.A. Nizami (ed), *Politics and Society During the early Medieval Period, Collected Works of Muhammad Habib*, 2 Vols., Delhi: People's Publishing House, 1974; Yusuf Husain, *Glimpses of Medieval Indian Culture,* Bombay: Asia Publishing House, 1957; K.A. Nizami, *Some Aspects of Religion and Politics in India During the 13th Centuries,* Aligarh: Aligarh Muslim University, 1961; S.A.A. Rizvi, *A History of Sufism in India, Vol. I, Early Sufism and its History in India to 1600 A.D.,* New Delhi: Munshiram Manoharlal, 1978; I.H. Siddiqui, 'The Early Chishti Dargahs', in C.W. Troll (ed), *Muslim Shrines in India – Their Character, History and Significance,* New Delhi: Oxford University Press, 1989.

9. *Siyar-ul-Auliya,* pp. 94-95; Shaikh Jamali. *Siyar-ul-Arifin,* Ms., IO Islamic 1313, OIOC, British Library, London., fol. 45b; Ali Asghar, *Jawahir-i-Faridi,* Lahore: Victoria Press, 1884, p. 220.
10. *Siyar-ul-Auliya,* pp. 64-65.
11. *Ibid.*, p. 145.
12. *Ibid.*, pp. 144-45; Sheikh Abdul Haqq Muhaddis Dehlawi, *Akhbar-ul-Akhyar,* Urdu translation by Subhan Mahmud and Muhammad Fazil, Delhi: Adabi Duniya, 1990, p. 64.
13. *Akhbar-ul-Akhyar,* pp. 63-64. For other accounts of the Alauddin Khalji's hostility towards the shaikh, his subsequent faith in the miraculous ability of the latter and acceptance of the princes, Khizr Khan and Shadi Khan, in the *jama'atkhana* as disciples of the shaikh, see Muhammad Jamal Qiwam, *Qiwam-ul-Aqa'id,* Urdu translation by Nisar Ahmad Faruqui, Rampur: Idarah Nashar-o-Isha'at, 1994, pp. 91-96. Also see Ziyauddin Barani, *Tarikh-i-Firuz-Shahi,* British Museum Ms. Or. 6376, OIOC, British Library, London, fols. 153a-b.
14. *Siyar-ul-Auliya,* pp. 255-56; *Akhbar-ul-Akhyar,* p. 87.

15. For a study of the 'authority' connotation of the shaikh's *wilayat*, leading to conflict with the rulers and the victory of the shaikh as recorded in the sources of the Delhi Sultanate, see Simon Digby, 'The Sufi Shaikh and the Sultan: A Conflict of Claims to Authority in Medieval India', *Iran – Journal of Persian Studies*, 1990, 28: 71-74.
16. Amir Hasan Sijzi, *Fawa'id-ul-Fu'ad*, Persian text with Urdu translation by Khwaja Hasan Sani Nizami, Delhi: Urdu Academy, 1991, Vol. IV, 21st meeting; *Siyar-ul-Auliya*, p. 89; *Tarikh-i-Firuz-Shahi*, fols. 158b-160a.
17. *Tarikh-i-Firuz-Shahi*, fols. 96b-99a.
18. *Akhbar-ul-Akhyar*, p. 79. For Abu Bakr Tusi, also see ibid., pp. 79-80. Among modern secondary works, see Nizami, *Religion and Politics in India*, pp. 288-91; Simon Digby, 'Qalandars and Related Groups: Elements of Social Deviance in the Religious Life of the Delhi Sultanate of the Thirteenth and Fourteenth Centuries', in Yohanan Friedmann (ed), *Islam in Asia, Vol. I, South Asia*, Jerusalem: Magness Press, 1984, pp. 67-68.
19. Of the four schools of Sunni jurisprudence, the Hanafites have been dominant in North Indian Islam. The Hanafite *ulama* of the Delhi Sultanate considered music assemblies organized by the shaikh illegal. The controversy surrounding Nizamuddin's justification of *sama* is discussed below. Also see, Bruce B. Lawrence, 'The early Chishti Approach to Sama', in M. Israel and N.K. Wagle (eds) *Islamic Society and Culture: Essays in Honour of Professor Aziz Ahmad*, Delhi: Manohar, 1983, pp. 69-93.
20. See, for example, the theologians' reaction to Shaikh Luqman Sarakhsi and his miraculous escape by riding a wall, *Fawa'id-ul-Fu'ad*, Vol. I, 7th meeting.
21. *Afzal-ul-Fawa'id*, collection of the discourses of Nizam-ud-

Din Auliya, compilation attributed to Amir Khusrau, Urdu trans., New Delhi: Maktaba Jam-i-Noor, n.d., p. 138.

22. *Siyar-ul-Arifin*, fols. 21b-22a.
23. See Richard M. Eaton, 'The Political and Religious Authority of the Shrine of Baba Farid', in Barbara D. Metcalf (ed), *Moral Conduct and Authority: The Place of Adab in South Asian Islam*, Berkley: University of California Press, 1984, pp. 333-56.
24. *Ibid.*, p. 75.
25. Minhaj-us-Siraj, *Tabaqat-i-Nasiri*, Vol I, edited by Abdul Hayy Habibi, Kabul: Anjuman Tarikh-i Afghanistan, 1963-64, pp. 441-42.
26. *Fawa'id-ul-Fu'ad*, Vol. IV, 61st meeting. For a different version of the account of bestowal of kingship to Iltutmish, see Nizam-ud-Din Ahmad, *Tabaqat-i-Akbari*, Ms. I.O. Islamic 3320, OIOC, British Library, London, fol. 28a. K.A. Nizami accepts these stories as true, *Studies in Medieval Indian History and Culture*, Allahabad: Kitab Mahal, 1966, p. 16; while Abbas Rizvi rejects them as myths, *History of Sufism in India*, p. 135, f.n.2.
27. Raziuddin Aquil, 'Sufi Cults, Politics and Conversion: The Chishtis of the Sultanate Period', *Indian Historical Review*, 1995-96, 22 (1-2), 190-97.
28. *Rahat-ul-Qulub,* collection of the discourses of Farid-ud-Din Ganj-i-Shakar, compilation attributed to Nizam-ud-Din Auliya', Urdu trans., Delhi: Maktaba Jam-i-Noor, n.d., p. 34; *Siyar-ul-Auliya*, p. 60; *Siyar-ul-Arifin*, fols. 34a-b. For the hostility between Qubacha and Zakariya, see *Fawa'id-Fu'ad*, Vol. IV, 4th meeting.
29. *Asrar-ul-Auliya,* collection of the conversations of Farid-ud-Din Ganj-i-Shakar compiled by Shaikh Badr-ud-Din Ishaq, Urdu trans. M. Muinuddin Durdai, Karachi: Nafis

Academy, 1975, pp. 183-84; *Fawa'id-us-Salikin*, p. 15; *Rahat-ul-Qulub*, p. 32.

30. *Fawa'id-ul-Fu'ad*, Vol. I, 8th meeting.
31. In Muslim folk-belief, the *pari* or fairy is reported to be a female *jinn*. Identified as companions of God and worshipped by the pre-Islamic Arabs, *jinns* have survived in Islamic societies as malevolent supernatural creatures. It is believed that there are two types of *jinns* – Muslim and infidel. The latter are supposed to be more wicked and difficult to be controlled. For a note on the places where they live, their behaviour towards human beings, particularly the illnesses afflicted by them, and the precautions taken to avoid falling in their trap, see the entry, 'Djinn', *The Encyclopaedia of Islam*, New Edition, Vol. II, Leiden: E.J. Brill, 1965, pp. 546-50.
32. Sudhir Kakar, *Shamans, Mystics and Doctors: A Psychological Inquiry into India and its Healing Traditions,* New Delhi: Oxford University Press, 1982, p. 29.
33. *Rahat-ul-Qulub*, pp. 16, 65, 87; *Fawa'id-ul-Fu'ad*, Vol. V, 29th meeting.
34. *Fawa'id-ul-Fu'ad*, Vol. IV, 51st meeting; Ibid., Vol. II, 17th meeting; *Siyar-ul-Auliya,* p. 96. For the later use of amulets among Muslims in India, see Jafar Sharif, *Islam in India or the Qanun-i-Islam – The Customs of the Muslamans of India*, trans. G.A. Herklots, revised by William Crooke, London, 1975, pp. 254-55.
35. Raziuddin Aquil, *Lovers of God: Sufism and the Politics of Islam in Medieval India*. New Delhi: Manohar, 2017.
36. *Qiwam-ul-Aqa'id*, pp. 33-35.
37. *Fawa'id-ul-Fu'ad*, Vol. IV, 3rd meeting. For the miracles of the Prophet, see A.J. Wensinck, 'Mu'djiza', *The Encyclopaedia of Islam*, New Edition, Vol. VII, Leiden: E.J. Brill, 1990, p. 295.

38. *Fawa'id-ul-Fu'ad*, Vol. IV, 44th meeting.
39. *Ibid.*, Vol. IV, 21st meeting; *Siyar-ul-Auliya*, p. 88.
40. *Fawa'id-ul-Fu'ad*, Vol. IV, 19th meeting.
41. *Khair-ul-Majalis*, 9th meeting.
42. *Fawa'id-ul-Fu'ad*, Vol. V, 2nd meeting.
43. *Ibid.*, Vol. IV, 26th meeting; *Siyar-ul-Arifin*, fols. 129a-130b.
44. For a detailed discussion of the activities of these deviant groups, their social background and the way they were treated by the Sufi shaikhs of different *silsilas*, see Digby, 'Qalandars and Related Groups', pp. 60-108.
45. Richard Eaton has questioned all these explanations in his, *The Rise of Islam and the Bengal Frontier, 1204-1760*, New Delhi: Oxford University Press, 1994, pp. 113-19.
46. This contrast has been noted in Nizami's numerous writings. See, for instance, *Religion and Politics*, pp. 177-80. See also Rizvi, *History of Sufism in India*, pp. 215-26.
47. See, for instance, S.A.A. Rizvi, *Muslim Revivalist Movements in Northern India in the 16th and 17th Centuries*, New Delhi: Munshiram Manoharlal, 1993, pp. 54-56; Mohammad Mujeeb, *Indian Muslims*, New Delhi: Munshiram Manoharlal, 1985, pp. 297-98.
48. Eaton, 'The Political and Religious Authority of the Shrine of Baba Farid in Pakpattan, Punjab'.
49. For a biographical sketch, see *Siyar-ul-Auliya*, pp. 54-55.
50. *Khair-ul-Majalis*, 11th meeting.
51. Jamali Kamboh, *Siyar-ul-Arifin*, Urdu trans. Ayub Qadiri, Lahore, 1976 [Hereafter *Siyar-ul-Arifin* (Urdu trans.)], pp. 6-8.
52. *Dalil-ul-Arifin*, Urdu trans., Delhi: Maktaba Jam-I-Noor, n.d., p. 57.
53. *Fawa'id-us-Salikin*, pp. 14-15.
54. *Asrar-ul-Auliya*, pp. 201-02.

55. *Siyar-ul-Auliya*, pp. 56-57.
56. *Siyar-ul-Arifin* (Urdu trans.), p. 14.
57. Abdul Haqq also notes that Pithaura was at Ajmer at the time of Mu'in-ud-Din's arrival there, *Akhbar-ul-Akhyar,* p. 22.
58. *Safinat-ul-Auliya*, p. 128. It is important to note that Dara Shukoh privileged his Qadiri order over the Chishtis.
59. *Siyar-ul-Auliya,* pp. 56-57.
60. For this and other references to the pilgrimage of Muinuddin Chishti's tomb in the 14th century, see Simon Digby, 'Early Pilgrimages to the Graves of Muinuddin Sijzi and other Chishti Shaikhs', in Israel and Wagle (eds), *Islamic Society and Culture*, pp. 95-100.
61. *Siyar-ul-Arifin* (Urdu trans.), pp. 14-15.
62. *Ibid.*, pp. 6-8, 14-16, 43-44.
63. See, for instance, Dara Shukoh, *Safinat-ul-Auliya*, Urdu trans. Muhammad Ali Lutfi, Delhi: n.d., pp. 127-28.

SELECT BIBLIOGRAPHY

Ahmad, Aziz. 1964. *Studies in Islamic Culture in Indian Environment,* Oxford: Clarendon Press.

Akhbar-ul-Akhyar of Shaikh Abdul Haqq Muhaddis Dehlawi. Ms., IO Islamic 1450, OIOC, British Library, London. Persian text edited by Alim Ashraf Khan. Tehran: Society for the Appreciation of Cultural Works and Dignitaries, 2005. Urdu translation by Subhan Mahmud and Muhammad Fazil, Delhi: Adabi Duniya, 1990.

Alakhbani, or *Rushdnama* (1971) of Abd al-Quddus Gangohi, Hindi translation by Saiyid Athar Abbas Rizvi and Shailesh Zaidi, Aligarh: Bharat Prakashan.

Alam, Muzaffar. 2009. "The Mughals, the Sufi Shaikhs and the Formation of the Akbari Dispensation," *Modern Asian Studies,* 43 (1): 166–73.

Alam, Muzaffar. 2011. "The Debate Within: A Sufi critique of Religious Law, *Tasawwuf* and Politics in Mughal India," *South Asian History and Culture,* 2 (2): 138–159.

Ansari, Zoe and Abul Faiz Sahar, eds. 1989. *Khusro Shanasi* Delhi: Taraqqi Urdu Bureau.

Aquil, Raziuddin, ed. 2010. *Sufism and Society in Medieval India,*

Debates in Indian History and Society Series, New Delhi: Oxford University Press.

Aquil, Raziuddin. 2007. *Sufism, Culture, and Politics: Afghans and Islam in Medieval North India*, New Delhi: Oxford University Press.

Aquil, Raziuddin. 2017a. *Lovers of God: Sufism and the Politics of Islam in Medieval India*, New Delhi: Manohar.

Aquil, Raziuddin. 2017b. *The Muslim Question: Understanding Islam and Indian History,* New Delhi: Penguin Random House.

Asher, Catherine B. and Cynthia Talbot. 2006. *India Before Europe,* Cambridge: Cambridge University Press.

Auer, Blain H. 2012. "Intersections between Sufism and Power: Narrating the Shaykhs and Sultans of Northern India, 1200-1400", in *Sufism and Society: Arrangements of the Mystical in the Muslim World, 1200-1800*, eds. John J. Curry and Erik S. Ohlander, London: Routledge.

Bashir, Shahzad. 2011. *Sufi Bodies: Religion and Society in Medieval Islam*, New York: Columbia University Press.

Behl, Aditya. 2014. "Emotion and Meaning in Mrigavat?: Strategies of Spiritual Signification in Hindavi Sufi Romances", Francesca Orsini and Samira Sheikh, eds., *After Timur Left: Culture and Circulation in Fifteenth-Century North India*, New Delhi: Oxford University Press.

Blair, Sheila S. 1990. "Sufi Saints and Shrine Architecture in the Early Fourteenth Century", *Muqarnas*, 7: 35–49.

Bokhari, Afshan. 2012. "Between Patron and Piety: Jahan Ara Begam's Sufi Affiliations and Articulations in the Seventeenth-Century Mughal India," in *Sufism and Society: Arrangements of the Mystical in the Muslim World, 1200-1800*, eds. John J. Curry and Erik S. Ohlander. London: Routledge, 120–42.

Brown, Katherine B. 2007. "Did Aurangzeb Ban Music? Questions for the Historiography of his Reign", *Modern Asian Studies*, 41 (1): 77–120.

Buehler, Arthur F. 2013. "Ahmad Sirhindi: Nationalist Hero, Good Sufi, or Bad Sufi?", in *South Asian Sufis: Devotion, Deviation, and Destiny*, eds. Clinton Bennett and Charles M. Ramsey, London: Bloomsbury, 141–62.

Busch, Allison. 2011. *Poetry of Kings: The Classical Hindi Literature of Mughal India*, New York: Oxford University Press.

Chandayan (2009) of Mulla Daud, A critical study by Naseem A. Hines, New Delhi: Manohar.

Chittick, William C. 2007. *Sufism: A Short Introduction,* Oxford: Oneworld Publications.

Clark, Matthew. 2016. "Religious Sects, Syncretism, and Claims of Antiquity: The Dashanami-Sannyasis and South Asian Sufis", in *Literary and Religious Practices in Medieval and Early Modern India,* edited by Raziuddin Aquil and David L. Curley, New Delhi and London: Manohar and Routledge.

Cornell, Vincent J. 2005. "Ibn Battuta's Opportunism: The Networks and Loyalties of a Medieval Muslim Scholar", in *Muslim Networks from Hajj to Hip Hop*, eds. Miriam Cooke and Bruce B. Lawrence, Chapel Hill: University of North Carolina Press, 31–50.

Currie, P.M. 1989.*The Shrine and Cult of Muin al-Din Chishti of Ajmer*, New Delhi: Oxford University Press.

Dale, Stephen F., *Babur: Timurid Prince and Mughal Emperor, 1483-1530*. New Delhi: Cambridge University Press.

De Bruijn, Thomas. 2012. *Ruby in the Dust: Poetry and History in Padmavat by the South Asian Sufi Poet Muhammad Jayasi*, Leiden: Leiden University Press.

Digby, Simon. 1983. "Early Pilgrimages to the graves of Muinuddin Sijzi and other Indian Chishti Shaikhs", in

Islamic Society and Culture – Essays in Honour of Aziz Ahmad, eds., M. Israel and N.K. Wagle, New Delhi: Manohar.

Digby, Simon. 1984. "Qalandars and Related Groups: Elements of Social Deviance in the Religious Life of the Delhi Sultanate of the Thirteenth and Fourteenth Centuries", in *Islam in Asia, Vol. I, South Asia,* ed., Yohanan Friedman, Jerusalem: Magnes, 67–68.

Digby, Simon. 1986. "The Sufi Shaykh as a Source of Authority in Medieval India", *Purushartha*, 9: 55–77.

Eaton, Richard M. 1978. *Sufis of Bijapur, 1300-1700: Social Roles of Sufis in Medieval India,* Princeton: Princeton University Press.

Eaton, Richard M. 1994. *The Rise of Islam and the Bengal Frontier,* New Delhi: Oxford University Press.

Eaton, Richard M., *Essays on Islam and Indian History,* New Delhi: Oxford University Press, 2002.

Ernst, Carl W. 1992. *Eternal Garden: Mysticism, History and Politics at a South Asian Sufi Centre,* Albany: State University of New York Press.

Ernst, Carl W. 2016. *Refractions of Islam in India: Situating Sufism and Yoga,* New Delhi: Sage/Yoda Press.

Ernst, Carl W. 2017. *It's Not Just Academic! Essays on Sufism and Islamic Studies,* New Delhi: Sage/Yoda Press.

Ernst, Carl W. and Bruce B. Lawrence. 2002. *Sufi Martyrs of Love: The Chishti Order in South Asia and Beyond,* New York: Palgrave Macmillan.

Faruqi, Ziya-ul-Hasan. 1996. *Fawa'id al-Fu'ad: Spiritual and Literary Discourses of Shaikh Nizamuddin Awliya/Originally Compiled by Amir Hasan 'Ala' Sijzi Dehlawi,* English translation with introduction and historical annotation. New Delhi: D.K. Printworld.

Faruqui, Munis D. 2014. "Dara Shukoh, Vedanta, and Imperial

Succession in Mughal India", in Munis D. Faruqui and Vasudha Dalmia, eds., *Religious Interactions in Mughal India*, New Delhi: Oxford University Press.

Fatawa-i-Jahandari (1972), by Ziya-ud-Din Barani, edited by Afsar Salim Khan, Lahore: Research Society of Pakistan.

Fawa'id-ul-Fu'ad (1990), Conversations of Shaikh Nizam-ud-Din Auliya, compiled by Amir Hasan Sijzi. Persian text with an Urdu translation by Khwaja Hasan Sani Nizami, Delhi: Urdu Academy.

Friedmann, Yohanan. 2003. "Islamic Thought in Relation to the Indian Context", in *India's Islamic Traditions, 711-1750*, ed., Richard M. Eaton, Delhi: Oxford University Press, 50–63.

Green, Nile. 2006. *Indian Sufism since the Seventeenth Century: Saints, Books and Empires in the Muslim Deccan*, London: Routledge.

Green, Nile. 2012. *Making Space: Sufis and Settlers in Early Modern India*, New Delhi: Oxford University Press.

Habib, Mohammad. 1974 and 1981. *Politics and Society during the Early Medieval Period: Collected Works of Mohammad Habib*, vols. 1-2, ed., K.A. Nizami, New Delhi: People's Publishing House.

Haqq, M. Enamul. 1975. *A History of Sufism in Bengal*, Dacca: Asiatic Society of Bangladesh.

Hawley, John S. 2015. *A Storm of Songs: India and the Idea of the Bhakti Movement*, Cambridge, MA: Harvard University Press.

Hawley, John S. and Kenneth E. Bryant. 2015. *Sur's Ocean: Poem's from the Early Tradition* (Murty Classical Library of India), Cambridge MA: Harvard University Press.

Jackson, Peter. 1999. *The Delhi Sultanate: A Political and Military History*, Cambridge: Cambridge University Press.

Jha, Mridula. 2016. "Mingling of the Oceans: A Journey through the Works of Dara Shikuh", in *Literary and Religious Practices in Medieval and Early Modern India*, edited by Raziuddin Aquil and David L. Curley, New Delhi and London: Manohar and Routledge.

Karamustafa, Ahmet T. 2007. *Sufism: The Formative Period,* The New Edinburgh Islamic Surveys, Edinburgh: Edinburgh University Press.

Khair-ul-Majalis (1959), Conversations of Shaikh Nasir-ud-Din Chiragh-i-Dehli, compiled by Hamid Qalandar, ed., K.A. Nizami, Aligarh: Muslim University.

Kugle, Scott. 2008. "The Accidental Revivalist: Abd al-Haqq Muhadith Dihlawi's Search for Islamic Knowledge and Power between Makka and Delhi", *Journal of Islamic Studies*, 19 (2): 196–246.

Kugle, Scott. 2016. "Sufi Attitude toward Homosexuality: Chishti Perspectives from South Asia", in *Literary and Religious Practices in Medieval and Early Modern India*, edited by Raziuddin Aquil and David L. Curley, New Delhi and London: Manohar and Routledge.

Kumar, Sunil. 2007. *The Emergence of the Delhi Sultanate, 1192-1286,* New Delhi: Permanent Black.

Lawrence, Bruce B. 1978. *Notes from a Distant Flute: The Extant Literature of Pre-Mughal Indian Sufism*. Tehran: Imperial Iranian Academy of Philosophy.

Lawrence, Bruce B. 1983. "The Early Chishti Approach to *Sama*", in *Islamic Society and Culture – Essays in Honour of Professor Aziz Ahmad,* eds., M. Israel and N.K. Wagle, New Delhi: Manohar, 69–93.

Lawrence, Bruce B. 1991. *Nizam Ad-Din Awliya: Morals for the Heart,* English translation of *Fawa'd-ul-Fu'ad*, New York: Paulist Press.

Lefevre, Corinne. 2014. "The Court of Abdur Rahim Khan-i Khanan as a Bridge Between Iranian and Indian Cultural

Traditions", in Allison Busch and Thomas de Brujin, eds, *Culture and Circulation in Premodern South Asia*, Leiden, 75–106.

Lorenzen, David N. 2010. *Nirgun Santonke Swapana*, New Delhi: Rajkamal Prakashan.

Lutgendorf, Philip. 2016. *The Epic of Ram* (Murty Classical Library of India), Cambridge MA: Harvard University Press.

Madhumalati (2000) of Mir Sayyid Manjhan Shattari Rajgiri, English translation by Aditya Behl and Simon Weightman, with Shyam Manohar Pandey, *Madhumalati: An Indian Sufi Romance*, New Delhi: Oxford University Press.

Mirza, M. Wahid. 1986. *Amir Khusrau*, Delhi: National Amir Khusrau Society.

Mukhia, Harbans. 2004. *The Mughals of India*, London: Blackwell.

Naim, C.M. 2004. *Urdu Texts and Contexts: The Selected Essays of C.M. Naim*, New Delhi: Permanent Black.

Nizami, K.A. 1955. *The Life and Times of Shaikh Fariduddin Ganj-i-Shakar*, Aligarh Aligarh: Muslim University.

Nizami, K.A. 1991a. *The Life and Times of Shaikh Nasiruddin Chiragh*, Delhi: Idarah-i-Adabiyat-i Delli.

Nizami, K.A. 1991b. *The Life and Times of Shaikh Nizamuddin Auliya*, Delhi: Idarah-i-Adabiyat-i Delli.

Novetzke, Christian Lee. 2008. *Religion and Public Memory: A Cultural History of Saint Namdev in India*, New York: Columbia University Press.

Orsini, Francesca, and Samira Sheikh, eds., 2014. *After Timur Left: Culture and Circulation in Fifteenth-Century North India*, New Delhi: Oxford University Press.

Orsini, Francesca. ed. 2010. *Before the Divide: Hindi and Urdu Literary Culture*. New Delhi: Orient Blackswan.

Padmavat (2010), of Malik Muhammad Jaisi, edited with commentary by Vasudev Sharan Agarwal, Allahabad: Lokbharti Prakashan.

Petevich, Carla. 2007. *When Men Speak as Women: Vocal Masquerade in Indo-Muslim Poetry*, New Delhi: Oxford University Press.

Qiwam al-'Aqa'id (1994), of Muhammad Jamal Qiwam, Urdu translation by Nisar Ahmad Faruqui. Rampur: Idarah Nashar-o-Isha'at.

Richards, J.F. 1991. *The Mughal Empire*, Cambridge: Cambridge University Press.

Rizvi, S.A.A. 1978. *A History of Sufism in India,* Vol. I. *Early Sufism and its History in India to 1600 AD*, Delhi: Munshiram Manoharlal.

Schimmel, Annemarie. 1978. *Mystical Dimensions of Islam*, Chapel Hill: University of North Carolina Press.

Sharma, Sunil. 2005. *Amir Khusraw: Poet of Sultans and Sufis*, Oxford: Oneworld Publications.

Siyar-ul-Arifin of Shaikh Jamali, Ms., IO Islamic 1313, OIOC, British Library, London.

Siyar-ul-Auliya (1978), of Amir Khwurd, Islamabad: Markaz Tahqiqat-i-Farsi Iran wa Pakistan.

Sreenivasan, Ramya, 2014a. "Warrior-Tales at Hinterland Courts in North India, 1370-1550", in Francesca Orsini and Samira Sheikh, eds., *After Timur Left: Culture and Circulation in Fifteenth-Century North India*, New Delhi: Oxford University Press

Sreenivasan, Ramya, 2014b. "Faith and Allegiance in the Mughal Era: Perspectives from Rajasthan", in Munis D. Faruqui and Vasudha Dalmia, eds., *Religious Interactions in Mughal India*, New Delhi: Oxford University Press.

Sreenivasan, Ramya. 2007. *The Many Lives of a Rajput Queen: Heroic Pasts in India, c. 1500-1900*. Seattle: University of Washington Press.

Suleiman Charitra (2015), of Kalyana Malla, English translation by A.N.D. Haksar, New Delhi: Penguin Books.

Syros, Vasileios. 2012. "An Early Modern South Asian Thinker on the Rise and Decline of Empires: Shah Wali Allah of Delhi, the Mughals, and the Byzantines", *Journal of World History*, 23 (4): 793–840.

Tarikh-i-Firuz Shahi of Ziya-ud-Din Barani, British Museum Ms. 6376, OIOC, British Library, London.

Tarikh-i-Mubarak Shahi (1931), of Yahya bin Ahmad bin Abdullah Sarhindi, edited by M. Hidayat Hosain. Calcutta: Asiatic Society.

Vanita, Ruth. 2012. *Gender, Sex and the City: Urdu Rekhti Poetry, 1780-1870*, New Delhi: Orient Blackswan.

Vaudeville, Charlotte. 1993. *A Weaver Named Kabir – Selected Verses with a Detailed Biographical and Historical Introduction*, Delhi: Oxford University Press.

Viitamaki, Mikko. 2016. "Retelling Medieval History for Twentieth-century Readers: Encounter of a Hindu Prince and a Sufi Master in Khwaja Hasan Nizami's *Nizami Bansuri*", in *Literary and Religious Practices in Medieval and Early Modern India*, edited by Raziuddin Aquil and David L. Curley, New Delhi and London: Manohar and Routledge.

Zaina Rajatarangi (1994), of Srivara, English translation by Kashinath Dhar. New Delhi: People's Publishing House.

Zutshi, Chitralekha. 2017. *Kashmir's Contested Pasts: Narratives, Sacred Geographies and the Historical Imagination*. New Delhi: Oxford University Press.

INDEX